HAUNTED CLWYD

RICHARD HOLLAND

GW00579585

Gwasg Carreg Gwalch

Text © Richard Holland 1992.

Copyright © by Gwasg Carreg Gwalch 1992.
All rights reserved. No part of this publication
may be reproduced or transmitted, in any form
or by any means, without permission.

ISBN: 0-86381-218-X

Cover design: Tim Pearce

First published in 1992 by
Gwasg Carreg Gwalch, 12 Iard yr Orsaf, Llanrwst, Wales LL26 0EH
☎ 01492 642031   ▤ 01492 641502
✉ books@carreg-gwalch.co.uk   Website: www.carreg-gwalch.co.uk

Printed in Wales

To Mike

— who almost got in

Also by Richard Holland — *Supernatural Clwyd;
the Folk Tales of North-East Wales*
(Gwasg Carreg Gwalch, 1989)

Contents

Preface 8

Abergele
Haunted castle; ball of fire 11

Acrefair
The tramp in the kiln; ghost evicts householders; the aqueduct 13

Afonwen
Oldest customer 16

Bronington
The lady vanishes 18

Broughton
Floating clergyman 19

Brymbo
The suicide 21

Bryneglwys
Vengeful beggar 22

Brynford
Horses' Leap; an Elizabethan 23

Bwlchgwyn
Phantom army 24

Caergwrle
Woman with no feet; black dog 25

Cefn Mawr
The woman on the bridge; "Annie"; smiling girl 27

Cerrigydrudion
The urgent voice 28

Chirk (**Y Waun**)
Cave of death; haunted flats 29

Cilcain
Shades of the Middle Ages 31

Colwyn Bay (**Bae Colwyn**)
Toys possessed; ghost of the bingo hall; evil laughter 33

Connah's Quay
Spectral hounds; the "horrible nun" 35

Corwen
Folorn lover; phantom funeral; ghosts of the chasm 37

Cwm
"John Henry" and a mysterious woman 39

Cymau
"Pray for my soul!"; a bad move 41

Denbigh (**Dinbych**)
The Goblin Tower; presence in the bookshop 43

Derwen
Giant's ghost 45
Efenechtyd
Apparitions of the future 46
Ewloe
A glowing figure, a singing voice and more 47
Flint
Tragic lovers; haunted hollow 49
Glyn Ceiriog
Spirits as servants; scream of terror 51
Gresford
Crisis apparition 52
Gwernymynydd
Old woman; giant silhouette 54
Halkyn (**Helygain**)
The ghost on the road 57
Hawarden (**Penarlâg**)
Gladstone's ghost; forbidden love; fighter pilot; the Glynne Arms 60
Henllan
Cold hands in bed 62
Holt
Cries of the drowned 64
Holywell (**Treffynnon**)
Spirited goings on at the Talacre Arms 65
Hope (**Caer Estyn**)
A lonely grave 67
Llanasa
The smell of thyme 68
Llanddulas
Haunting housekeeper 69
Llandegla
Violent entities 70
Llangernyw
The recording angel; bloody conflict 72
Llangollen
The Ladies; Owain Glyndŵr; a remarkable vision; an unknown visitor . 74
Llangynhafal
The miserly squire 76
Llannefydd
Murderous Mam Cymru 77
Llanrhaeadr-yng-Nghinmeirch
Incorruptible corpse; wicked Dafydd Salusbury;
a house "too haunted" 79

Llantysilio
The spirits' prophecy 82
Llanynys
The Jew's grave 84
Marford
The Lady Blackbird 86
Mold (**Yr Wyddgrug**)
Disturbances at No. 4; the clutching horror; startled awake;
man in a cap; shadow of the past; haunted chippy;
spirit after hours; spectre of a murder; King of the Hill;
the goblin well 88
Mynydd Hiraethog
The centurion's curse 98
Mynydd Isa
Two figures and a dog; the warning whistle 99
Nannerch
Death at a glance; the woman in black 102
Pentrefoelas
The Squire of Foelas; a phantom pig 105
Pontblyddyn
Clwyd's most famous haunted house 107
Prestatyn
Ghosts of Nant Hall Road; the white nun 108
Rhes-y-cae
The Cursed Skull 110
Rhewl
Ghosts' treasure; goblin army 112
Rhos-on-Sea (**Llandrillo-yn-Rhos**)
The Monk's Kitchen 113
Rhuddlan
Demon of the castle; the ghost with the broad-brimmed hat;
the grinning horrors 115
Rhyl
Waving out to sea 117
Rossett
Left to rot 118
Ruabon (**Rhiwabon**)
Twilight cortege; legends of the column 120
Ruthin (**Rhuthun**)
The axe murderess 122
St Asaph (**Llanelwy**)
The Bodeugan poltergeist 125

Shotton
Schoolmam 127
Trefnant
Death on the road 128
Trelawnyd
Boudicca's grave 129
Treuddyn
The exorcist's greatest challenge; the soldier's Bible 130
Wrexham (**Wrecsam**)
Ghost in the machines; the sadler; burnt to death;
room full of smoke; walled up alive; St Richard Gwyn?;
disco monk; the Hanging Judge; dancing druids; drowning man;
floating lumps; horrible death of the Squire of Borras 132
Bibliography 138

Preface

What does the word "ghost" conjure up for you? A shrouded figure, dragging chains folornly through a mouldering graveyard? A creature of folklore, or a delusion, or a chance trick of the light? The truth, I have found, is rather different.

I have found that the least likely haunt of a ghost is a graveyard. More likely it is the front room of a cosy home, or it is a shop, or a bingo hall, or a village street. For every haunted castle one can find a haunted semi. The phantom monk of Rhos-on-Sea, for example, regularly haunted not the grounds of some ruined abbey, but the homely confines of a tea-shop, and the nun of Prestatyn takes her afterlife strolls along the breezy seafront!

What impresses one most when investigating ghost stories is how disarmingly commonplace they seem to be, and how matter-of-fact the witnesses. It seems everyone has seen a ghost — or knows someone who has. And for each the experience has been a unique, a personal thing. Perhaps a chance encounter on the stairs with a man in old-fashioned costume; or the cry of a disembodied voice below the window; a glimpse out of the corner of the eye; or the terrifying appearance of a loved one at the moment of their death. Take the contrast of the homes of Geoff Ellis of Mynydd Isa, where his young child plays with a friendly phantom dog, and of Siân Roadhouse of Mold, where a malignant, formless thing lurks in the dark, waiting to attack her in her bed and drag her out with invisible fingers tightly grasping her shoulders . . .

Contained within these pages is a host of haunts from Clwyd, incomplete, as it needs had to be, but representative and fascinating. The tales have been culled from many sources: from the county's rich heritage of folklore, from the many books on the subject, old and new, from newspaper reports, from letters I have received from readers of my *History and Mystery* column in local newspapers and *Country Quest* magazine, and, most importantly of all, from eye-witnesses, first-hand.

At this point I would like to offer my thanks to everyone who has helped with the making of this book, especially to the staff of the Clwyd Library Service and the County Records office for their usual courtesy and efficiency, to the many people who kindly agreed to allow me to recount their experiences, and to Tim, Tim and Alan for the necessary driving about.

I hope that this book, as a companion to my previous *Supernatural Clwyd* (Gwasg Carreg Gwalch, 1989), will help to establish that this beautiful, secret land we now call Clwyd is not only the gateway to Wales, but also a gateway to special mystery . . .

Sinister stone head in the garden wall of the haunted terrace, Mold

Abergele

There can scarcely be more romantic a setting for a haunting than Gwrych Castle, near Abergele, on the coast. A fabulous, fairy-tale folly, Gwrych was built in 1820 by Lloyd Bamford Hesketh to replace his old, crumbling family home down on the shore. High imposing walls line the road, hiding the castle from prying eyes, and isolated towers perched on the limestone cliffs lend added drama to the scene.

Despite its comparatively recent age, I have heard rumours of the ghost of a Civil War soldier being seen here in full 17th century costume and a few years ago a woman wrote into my *History and Mystery* column in the *Rhyl Journal* newspaper to say that she had seen near the castle a white lady wearing a gown and a long, pointed hat with a veil, "like a knight's lady." The stables, too, are reputedly haunted and there is said to be a cursed room.

However, Gwrych's best authenticated ghost is that of the Red Lady, who has frequently been seen roaming the grounds at dusk. The boxer, Bruce Woodcock, encountered the Red Lady while he was spending some time at the castle in training for his world title fight against Lee Savold in 1950. Mr Woodcock was out taking an evening stroll, when, on turning a corner, he came across a lady in a long red dress sitting by the side of the path, weeping. He had never seen the woman before, and so was momentarily taken aback. Then he enquired: "Anything wrong, miss?"

She did not reply, so he approached to see if he could be of assistance. He was within five feet of her, when she suddenly disappeared!

The Red Lady's identity is a mystery. Some say that she is the shade of a woman killed when thrown from a horse during a fox hunt — hence her red riding habit. Others have it that she is a past owner of the castle who was so in love with it that she demanded that she be buried within its grounds. Her wish was complied with, but because the land is unconsecrated, she cannot rest.

Like a fairy-tale, the romantic towers of Gwrych Castle, rise from the woodlands near Abergele

The road below the castle also has its ghosts. An old woman who suddenly evaporates into thin air has been frequently seen. A mysterious "ball or wheel of fire" was also observed several times, many years ago, hurtling along this road, disappearing as quickly as it had appeared. This strange apparition may commemorate the raging fires of a railway disaster which took place nearby in 1868.

Acrefair

At night the country above the village of Acrefair, near Wrexham, can seem an eerie one. The landscape is pock-marked by the remains of old pottery works, tips, cuttings and ruined kilns, and these form dark hollows and cast odd shadows. Today it is silent but a century ago the scene was quite different, the site of one of the most productive pottery works in Europe, famous for the quality of its wares. One of the many crumbling kilns one can find as one rambles around the overgrown ruins hides a dark secret. It was the scene of a gruesome tragedy, which led to an unusual and particularly disturbing haunting.

At the height of its industry, the area became the begging ground of a tramp, who would receive bits of bread from the workers and take advantage of the warmth of a kiln to bed down in for the night. One bitter winter's evening, the tramp, as usual, chose for himself a kiln and curled up in it and went to sleep. It was the last night he was to spend on earth . . .

The kiln had already been loaded with the square blocks of clay to make the bricks and it was ready for firing. The following morning the workers came to light the kiln, but because he was hidden behind the clay blocks, they did not see the tramp asleep there. They closed the kiln's heavy doors and fired it up. The old man instantly woke up, flames flaring out from the floor all around him, and he struggled through the smoke to the doors — but he found them locked. He hammered upon the doors but they were too thick for his knocking to be heard and his faint cries for help went also unheeded as the workers walked away to see about their work at the next kiln.

Hours later, the men returned to discover the remains of the tramp's body behind the bricks, charred almost beyond recognition. Blackened, bony fingers clutched the clay, telling of the tramp's agony in death.

Soon after the tragedy, a shadowy shape was regularly seen flitting around the kiln and muffled screams could sometimes be heard coming from within it. But most distressing of all, for five and even ten years afterwards, bricks would be removed from it which bore deep fingermarks embedded in the clay!

Thomas Telford's masterwork, the Froncysyllte aqueduct, carries the Shropshire Union Canal high above the valley of the Dee

The above story was collected as part of a project a friend of mine, Kath Wilkinson, a teacher at Ruabon High School, ran with her fourth year English class. She asked them to gather ghost stories from the area and they came up with many fascinating tales, many told them by elderly relatives. One site particularly favoured as being haunted was the Pontcysyllte Aqueduct, which unites Acrefair's neighbouring villages of Trevor and Froncysyllte.

The aqueduct, one of the most popular tourist attractions in Clwyd, was built by Thomas Telford between 1795 and 1805 to carry the Shropshire Union Canal. 120 feet high and 1007 feet long, with 19 arches, the aqueduct commands fine views of the Dee Valley, and barges regularly still use it.

According to tradition, many men were killed and suffered injury during the aqueduct's construction. Without today's modern machinery, it fell to men to lift heavy, bulky materials, and to fit them at precarious heights. Many accidents occurred. It is for this reason, say the children, that a white figure is seen to cross the aqueduct at night. It is the ghost of one of the many men who sacrificed his life for Telford's masterpiece. Visit Pontcysyllte at midnight, they say, and you are sure to see him.

Afonwen

The Pwllgwyn Hotel at Afonwen can perhaps boast the oldest customer of any hostelry in Wales — for he may date back as far as Medieval times! The Pwllgwyn once catered for pilgrims to the famous St Winifred's Well at Holywell, and landlady Beryl Bennion believes that it is one of these devout souls who occasionally is still to be seen sitting at a table in the dining room, dressed in a monk's habit, leaning on his elbows as if deep in thought. The first time Mrs Bennion saw the monk, she mistook him for a living patron:

"He just looked so real," she explained. "I thought you could see through ghosts, but he was as solid as anything. He was sitting right by the window, so I could see him clearly — but the rest of the room was dark, and my first reaction was annoyance at my staff for leaving what I thought to be a customer unattended. So, I hurried out and scolded one of the girls and told her to go in and see to him. But, of course, she came back all perplexed. She hadn't been able to see anyone in the room, and when I returned he'd completely disappeared!"

The monk has been seen on and off for years by visitors to the Pwllgwyn. Another apparition, a more shadowy figure, has been observed by husband Ray Bennion, who told me:

"It was about 6.30 one evening and I came down to open the bar. At the bottom of the stairs I put on some lights and then went to put the fire on, and I saw a person standing by the bar. I thought, how'd he get in? But suddenly he wasn't there at all! I thought at first it must have been a trick of the light, but a little later, after the bar was open, but empty, and all the lights were on, I saw him again. I was reading but became aware of a figure standing by the other end of the bar. I looked up but he'd gone — and I got a cold feeling all over . . ."

The other ghost of the Pwllgwyn is said to be a woman — her history unknown — who haunts the upstairs rooms. This may explain the cheeky — and unnerving — experience Ray had one evening while doing some bookwork in his lounge. He had been standing at a table when he felt a hand slip into his pocket!

"This is a habit my wife has when she wants some money!" said Ray. "But when I turned round to tell her off, there was nobody there — and the door was shut. It really frightened me, I don't mind telling you. I didn't go upstairs again all night!"

Bronington

Bronington is a peaceful village south of Wrexham, in the Maelor Saesneg, a pastoral corner of the county, bordering Salop and very English in character. In the Clwyd Record Office, Hawarden, I came across a Victorian preacher's book belonging to the Rev. Matthew Henry Lee, the then Vicar of Hanmer. Among the lists of hymns sung, sermons read, and funds raised, were several accounts of ghost sightings, including one from Bronington. I quote the entry:

"George Metcalf of Moss Lane (leading to Cuckoo's Nook) in Bronington, who was born about 1821, told me on Friday September 19th 1884, that as he was going for Welsh Coals in 1844 August he saw before him in the Wrexham Road, where the Pandy Toll Bar afterwards stood, the figure of a woman in a light-coloured dress, with a Tuscan bonnet, and some broad ribbon, which fell upon the left shoulder and waved in the wind. She held up her dress with her right hand, and wore low black shoes. He intended asking her to ride in the cart, and taking his eyes off her for a moment to hasten the horses, she was nowhere to be seen. This happened about 4.30 a.m."

The Rev. Lee, later Canon of St Asaph as well as vicar of Hanmer, clearly had an interest in the paranormal, for scribbled on the lower margin of one page was the address of the then newly-formed Society For Psychical Research!

Canon Lee became something of a local celebrity a few years later when he courageously saved the parish registers and plate from his beautiful and ancient church when it was gutted by fire in 1889. A "hurrican" was blowing and the fire brigade could not reach the blaze, which had been started by faulty heating equipment. Wrapped in wet sheets, Canon Lee took it upon himself to enter the burning building, at considerable personal risk. Although he survived the inferno, his health was seriously impaired afterwards, and sadly he died a year later.

Broughton

The Old Warren at Broughton is a sparse and lonely area of country, now bounded by the new Chester bypass. Before this bypass was built, the Old Warren road led to Buckley, but it has now been truncated and leads nowhere. Years ago this road was patrolled by an eerie phantom which had the habit of frightening young couples.

A Buckley resident, who lived in Broughton as a girl, told me that her parents saw the ghost when they were courting. It was a late evening one year in the early 1930's and my informant's parents, then young lovers, were returning arm-in-arm down the road. The road was heavily wooded then and very dark, which is what made it such a favourite place for courting couples. Suddenly they noticed a strange figure approaching them, taller than anyone they had ever seen. As it drew near they saw it was an old man, very thin, dressed in black and with a broad-brimmed hat, like an old-fashioned clergyman's, on his head. Then they realised there was something very unearthly about him — he wasn't walking but gliding! His feet weren't on the ground. There was no sound of footsteps, or any other sound from him at all. He just glided past, his gaunt face impassive, looking neither to right nor left. The young couple went cold all over, and hurried home as fast they could. A few years later there was another witness:

"My mam's younger sister, my auntie, saw the same apparition on the road when she was courting," my informant explained. "Her future husband had a motorbike, and they were standing by it, saying goodnight, when this same figure came gliding past. As he floated by, the bike's lights suddenly came on! They dimmed again after he had passed by. Well, they just jumped on the bike and rode away!"

She continued: "I can also recall an old man saying to my grandad he'd just seen a ghost, and it sounded like the same one, so it seems as though other people had seen it too. I don't know the story behind the ghost. I remember my mam had some idea he was the ghost of an old rector from one of the local churches. But, whoever, he was apparently very frightening to look at. He was so tall, almost impossibly so. And the way he glided along without a sound was enough to make anyone shiver!"

The creepy clergyman does not seem to have been encountered for some years, but perhaps now that the bypass has made the Old Warren quiet again, he will continue his perambulations and once again take to startling young lovers in his prudish — and otherworldly — way.

Brymbo

Some might say that the real ghost of Brymbo is its steelworks, closed in 1990 after nearly 200 years of production. The Old Number One furnace at the works had been smelting iron since 1803. Also a thing of the past is stately Brymbo Hall; it was demolished in the 1950's. Prior to that date it was haunted by the presence of a young girl, who killed herself to avoid an arranged marriage.

The woman was engaged to wed a man she did not love, and she despaired at the thought of sharing her future life with him. On her 21st birthday, at a grand ball held in her honour, the girl suddenly burst into tears and hurried away from the assembled guests, leaving behind confusion and wagging tongues.

She ran to a little room near the roof, where she had spent many solitary hours secretly weeping. There, in her misery, she hanged herself. The gossiping guests waited in vain for her return, but as she did not reappear, a maid was sent in search for her. The poor girl's scream on discovering the body sliced through the house, abruptly silencing their chattering.

From that day on, Brymbo Hall was a house of unrest. Doors would open of their own accord and gusts of icy air would blast through. The room where the girl hanged herself became known as "the haunted room". Dogs would not enter it and the windows in the room would never stay closed. Even if they were fastened with string they would be found open again the next morning.

The ghost also took to haunting the road leading up to the hall — renamed "The Ghost Road". Travellers on the road would feel sudden chills and invisible hands plucking at their coats. Locals still report a ghost being seen occasionally on this road, but, interestingly enough, it is now described as "an old woman."

Bryneglwys

One of the most enigmatic figures in old Clwyd tales is the Rev. Griffiths, of Llanarmon-yn-Iâl. According to the stories, the Rev. Griffiths was a renowned layer of ghosts, an exorcist. We know very little of him historically, but he seems to have been the stuff of legend, for in any local tale of the laying of a ghost, it is Griffiths who is named as the hero, and he has been specially sent for, his reputation known.

One account, from the Rev. Elias Owen's *Welsh Folk-Lore*, published in 1896, tells how Griffiths exorcised a ghost from Tŷ Mawr Farm at Bryneglwys. The Tŷ Mawr ghost was the spirit of an old tramp who had called at the farm one bitter winter's night begging food and shelter. The servant girls, amused at his shabby appearance, had scorned him and sent him away.

"You shall repent your conduct to me!" he admonished them, before retreating into the freezing night. The next morning the tramp's stiff body was found under one of the hedges on the farm, frozen to death. And then the trouble started . . .

The servants who had sent the poor man away were tormented night and day by the spirit. It harrassed them constantly, invisible hands pinched at their flesh and they were never given a moment's peace, until they were tired of their lives.

The Rev. Griffiths was called, and he drew two magic circles on the floor of the kitchen. He stood in one and charged the vengeful spirit to materialise in the other. He engaged in a mighty struggle of wills with the spirit, but eventually gained mastery over it, weakening it progressively until it was reduced from an awesome, frightening entity down to the harmless form of a spider, wriggling impotently in the circle. Swiftly, the Rev. Griffiths snapped the spider up in a tobacco tin he had in his pocket. The spirit wriggled furiously inside, but could not escape. Griffiths attached a stone to the tin, and dropped it into a bog on Llandegla Moors, trapping the entity there forever. It never returned to plague the inhabitants of Tŷ Mawr.

For further tales of the Rev. Griffiths' exploits, see under Llandegla and Treuddyn.

Brynford

Brynford, south of Holywell, is situated on the north side of desolate Halkyn Mountain, a windswept ex-mining area, where coarse grass and shrub struggle to maintain a foothold on hummocks of mine heaps poisoned with lead.

Near the village are two standing stones, their origin a mystery. Some say they mark a Bronze Age or early Christian grave, but they are not officially recognised as an ancient monument. Their name is Naid-y-March, or the *Horse's Leap*'.

Here, on moonlit nights, a phantom horseman has been seen, apparently searching for something. A local resident found an ancient sword, some bones and shoe soles near his shed and believes they may have belonged to the horseman, and it is these that he is searching for.

Another legend is that the horse's leap was made in the 16th century by a nobleman who fell from his mount during the attempt and broke his neck. It is his ghost, they say, which haunts the site.

South of Brynford is the Elizabethan Llwynerddyn Hall, haunted, apparently, by its original owner. In 1973, Mr and Mrs Kynaston owned the house, and started a programme of restoration with a grant from the Royal Commission. It was then that the figure of a man in Elizabethan costume, complete with ornate ruff, began to make its presence known.

Mrs Kynaston saw him at least six times. On one occasion he was sitting at the top of the stairs in an old chair her husband had bought for a few pence and restored. Said Mrs Kynaston, in an interview with the *Evening Leader* newspaper:

"The sun was just setting and the sky was all red. I was walking up the stairs when I saw him sitting there as clear as a real person. He looked very contemplative."

Mr Kynaston also saw the ghost, while repairing the floor of an upstairs room. A grey figure passed him and went through the wall where a door used to be. The couple soon got used to the presence. It would telegraph its appearance by a sudden drop in room temperature, whereupon the family dogs would beat a hasty exit from the room!

Bwlchgwyn

At Bwlchgwyn, near Wrexham, is a deep wooded valley, Nant-y-Ffrith, a great gash in the earth caused by a massive geological fault. Here in the 17th century an amazing sight was witnessed: literally a whole army of ghosts.

The vision was recorded by the historian Robert Parry as taking place in September 1602. There is no explanation for the phantoms, no historical event to which they might belong, and yet they were watched for some time by many witnesses. Here is Robert Parry's description of the event:

"About this time was seane about Nant-y-Ffrith . . . in the edge of the eveninge to the nomber of 2 or 3 thousande armed men a hors backe with banners displayed marchinge in warlike maner where as indeed there was no such thinge but some apparition or forewarninge of liklyhoode. And yet that was verefyed by 8 or ixen persons some of them credyte that all iontly saw the same."

Caergwrle

For such a small town, Caergwrle has a very long history. The probable site of a Roman station, Caergwrle is dominated by its ruined Medieval castle, which has recently undergone extensive excavations. In the 19th century, it was an important spa town, with many from a wide area coming to try its medicinal springs, now sadly overgrown. Up until recent years it was popular with people from Merseyside as a place for day-outs, and many of Caergwrle's older residents settled here on their retirement, attracted by memories of the many pleasant days they spent picnicking within the castle walls.

It would be surprising if such an historic and busy place didn't have one or two ghosts to boast of. A long-time resident of the town saw the phantom of a little old lady in Victorian costume some years ago. She described her sighting in an interview on BBC Radio Clwyd.

"I'd been playing tennis and was coming home about 10 o'clock at night down by the back of the castle," she explained. "There used to be a door at the bottom, and what should come out of there but a little old lady.

"She had a nice black cloak on and a black hat like a Salvation Army bonnet, but the thing I couldn't get over was that she had no feet! She was moving on air.

"So, I got on my tip-toes to go and see where she was going, and she went through the side gate. The next morning I went to have a look at the old door at the bottom of the castle, and it was all locked with a great big rusty bolt on it."

The same woman also saw a mysterious black dog roaming the street one night. It came bounding over the castle wall and straight under her feet. It was something like a labrador. The woman's companion sharply enquired why she had pulled back suddenly.

"Well, don't tread on the dog," she replied, and watched it cross the road and into the ditch on the other side. But her companion could see nothing.

Supernatural black dogs are very much a part of Welsh folklore. Gwyllgi, or Dogs of Darkness, are giant shaggy animals with glowing red eyes. I described some encounters with these frightening apparitions in my *Supernatural Clwyd*. However, the homely labrador in this case appears to have simply been the ghost of someone's pet.

Cefn Mawr

One of the many mining communities which grew up around Wrexham in the 19th century, Cefn Mawr is the setting for another tale gleaned from the children of Ruabon High School. My young informant tells me that a friend of her great-grandmother, a miner at the Green Colliery, was walking to work early one morning along the railway bridge above the quarry, when he saw approaching him a woman with a shawl over her head. To his horror, he saw the woman climb up onto the parapet of the bridge as though she were going to jump! He leapt forward to prevent her — but she vanished! He was so upset, he went home, and told his wife all about it.

An hour later he heard the awful whine of the hooter coming from the pit . . . There had been an accident, and three men on his shift had been killed. If he hadn't encountered the mysterious figure on the bridge, he could very well have been one of the victims! Was the apparition a warning from beyond the grave, in order to save his life?

The children also tell me that a house near the library is haunted by "Annie," a young girl who was made to live in the attic. One night she fell down the stairs and was killed. Some nights, say the children, you can hear her screaming.

At nearby Rhosymedre, a little girl in Victorian costume haunts some flats, according to the grandmother of one of the pupils, who would frequently see her. She had long black hair and wore a frilly knee-length dress and black boots.

"She always used to smile at my nanna and disappear," I was told. "My uncle went to visit and he saw this little girl and was very frightened. Apparently, in the 1800s there used to be a big house, with three or four daughters. The house burnt down and in its place was built my nanna's flats."

Cerrigydrudion

Ghosts, like the ideal small children in the saying, are usually seen but not heard; it is very rare for them to speak. However, occasionally the opposite is true, the ghost being no more than a disembodied voice, speaking out of the darkness, accompanied by no visible form. Such a phantom was experienced by a Dr Davies of Cerrigydrudion last century. One bitter winter's night he was awoken from his well-earned rest by a voice calling his name beneath his window. Drowsily, he lay in bed listening awhile, unsure whether he had dreamt it. Then it came again, entreating him to come to Craigyrychen farm on the moors. Dr Davies rose and went to the window. He peered out through the frosted glass but could see no-one, so returned to his bed. He was reluctant to answer the call, for the farm was a full three miles away, up a poor, muddy track which made journeying difficult at the best of times. In such harsh weather, in the middle of the night, the very idea made him shudder.

For a third time, however, the voice called up to him, and this time its urgent tone roused him to action. He opened the window and shouted down that he would follow the messenger shortly. He did not see anyone below, but assumed that whoever it was had headed home to prepare for his arrival. It took Dr Davies a long while to reach Craigyrychen in the pitch darkness, battling against wind and freezing rain, but as he drew near, he saw that all the lights in the farmhouse were lit — a sure sign of something amiss. He urged his horse to gee up and, grabbing his small black bag, he hurried into the farmhouse.

He was surprised by the unexpected welcome he received. He found that the farmwife was in labour, about to give birth, and there were complications — she swiftly needed medical attention. But the doctor discovered that no-one from the farm had sent for him. The farmer explained that they had considered it far too treacherous a night to risk sending anyone out for him, or to ask him to make the journey himself. No-one could have known of the troubles at Craigyrychen but the family themselves. The owner of the anxious voice calling for Dr Davies' presence remained a mystery — but thanks to it, the life of a young mother, and her baby, were saved.

Chirk

Chirk Castle, built by Edward I as one of a chain to help control the Welsh Border, is one of the oldest inhabited castles in Wales. Its original owners were the Mortimer family, whose emblem, a red hand, figures prominently on the impressive 18th century wrought iron gates at the entrance to the park. An old story says that the Mortimers were made to display a bloody hand as a symbol of their cruelty.

Near the castle is the entrance to a cave which is said to stretch under the hills all the way to Llanymynech, south of Oswestry. This cave, which was a Roman mining level, has a sinister reputation.

It is said that if anyone went within five paces of its entrance, they would find themselves drawn into it and would become lost inside its catacombs forever. A fox, chased by a hunt, once tried to hide in it, but was so scared by something it saw that it shot out again, right into the middle of the pack of hounds. They let it be, however, because it smelt so strongly of brimstone!

One Hallowe'en, a fiddler by the name of Iolo ap Huw decided to prove the cavern's extent by walking from the Llanymynech end to the Chirk opening, playing the fiddle as he went. He provided himself with an immense amount of bread and cheese and 7lbs of candles, and striking up a tune, entered the yawning entrance. He was never seen alive again.

However, many years later, a shepherd passing close by the cave's mouth at twilight heard the strains of a violin coming from within. Then an appalling apparition revealed itself — Iolo ap Huw, playing the fiddle like the Devil, his face white, his head lolling about on his shoulders, only the frenzied movement of his arms keeping him upright.

The traveller stared with a numb horror, then the apparition vanished back into the cave, "dragged inwards like the smoke up a chimney."

Many years later, one December Sunday, the shepherd was sitting in church with the congregation when he heard the sound of a fiddle playing beneath the church. He recognised it as the tune Iolo's spirit had been performing.

According to another story, a bagpiper entered the cave with the same intention as Iolo, but the pipes stopped halfway and the piper never emerged.

A more recent, and it might be said more frightening, account of a haunting is reported by ghost hunter extraordinaire Peter Underwood in his *Ghosts of Wales* (Christopher Davies, 1978). Near the castle once stood some wooden flats, formerly a Prisoners of War camp. The place possessed a brooding atmosphere, with the residents feeling that they were being constantly watched by some unseen presence. They would also find themselves suffering from reasonless bouts of depression or would wake up in the night suddenly, inexplicably, afraid.

During the 1950s the hauntings were at their height. Mysterious sounds would be heard in the flats, sometimes accompanied by strange smells, and taps would frequently turn themselves on or off with no-one near them. Then the ghosts were seen: an extraordinary array of them, most half-formed but others more solid; a lady which may have been a nun or a nurse, a man with a white stick, and a figure resembling a bishop. Strange angel-like shapes were also seen and terrifying pale faces stared out of the darkness.

Loud rappings and rustlings sometimes accompanied the ghosts. When a man lit a cigarette in an empty room to calm his nerves a voice out of nowhere asked him for one.

A seance was held, and apparently contacted the spirits of an Italian prisoner of war who had died of pneumonia and a woman who had given most of her rations to the sick prisoners, and so constantly smoked to quell her hunger.

Eventually, people refused to live at the flats, and they were demolished.

Cilcain

One of the most fascinating old buildings in Clwyd is the isolated Brithdir Mawr, which stands beside an ancient track on the lower slopes of Moel Fama, overlooking Loggerheads and Cilcain. Built in the 14th century, it underwent some small alterations in the 16th century and has been scarcely touched since. It is a very rare example of a Medieval hall house remarkably preserved.

In 1987, when I visited Brithdir Mawr, it was the home of Jane Mould — and also of a woman who had died during the Middle Ages, but who continued to be seen around the house. Jane never saw her, but some friends of hers staying for a dinner party did, standing by the entrance to the kitchen, in a long blue dress and a wimple. She has most often been encountered in the master bedroom, which is used for paying guests. A

The ancient seat of Brithdir Mawr keeps its secrets in a secluded spot, tucked away in a fold of the Clwydian Range of hills

woman saw the figure standing over her husband's bed one night, and then walking through a walled-up door

A spectral smell, as of something cooking, is the most frequent "ghost" at Brithdir Mawr, however.

"It's wonderful," said Jane, "very savoury, like stew. It makes you hungry just to smell it! I often come across it in the passageway."

Jane remembers that previous owners, who lived at the hall between 1920 and 1958, also once saw what may have been Medieval huntsmen riding down the track.

Colwyn Bay

"It's very scary," were the words one young assistant used to describe the Poundstretcher shop in Colwyn Bay. For here a whole host of inexplicable poltergeist-type phenomena broke out, terrifying the girls who worked there.

Toys allegedly "went mad," suitcases fell from shelves with no-one near them, lights dimmed and flickered and wash basins would be found unexpectedly full of water. Shop boss Karl Jones was dismissive of these reported happenings, however.

"I do not believe in ghosts," he told the *Evening Leader* newspaper, "it's just that the shop is an old building and when the floorboards creak or there is a strange sound, the girls think it's a ghost."

Nevertheless, a medium was later brought in and apparently banished the ghost. There seems no explanation for the visitation, but there is some mystery attached to the shop, for many years ago, when it was a department store, the owner vanished without trace and was never heard of again . . .

At the Princess Theatre Bingo and Social Club it's a case of haunted housey-housey! Strange noises and the occasional fleeting figure have frightened staff members after closing time. On Hallowe'en night, 1990, manageress Mrs Sandra Lloyd took several snapshots in the club at the end of the night — and on one of them, after development, a misty figure was revealed, hovering over a barman. The photo was published in the *County Pioneer* and Mrs Lloyd told the paper that she had seen nothing unusual when she had taken it.

"I cannot explain what it is," Mrs Lloyd was quoted as saying, "but the place is reputed to be haunted. It used to be a cinema and there are stories that a projectionist was accidentally killed in the projection box."

When a young couple bought an old travelling trunk at an antiques shop they brought into their Old Colwyn home a terrifying entity. Shortly after the old trunk was brought into the house, the couple's small son suddenly screamed out from his bedroom. His mother found him sitting up in bed, white-faced and sweating. He explained that he had woken up to find a strange man sitting on the end of his bed laughing at him. She comforted the child as best she could, but was uneasy — a little while before, she too had heard the sound of laughter, cruel and mocking, coming from an empty corner of the living room.

After the couple had retired to bed, a grey, cloudy object suddenly materialised in the room, enveloping the woman. At the same time, a great weight seemed to press down on the bed. The young woman felt bitterly cold, and she felt something brush up against her. Her husband quickly turned on the light — but there was nothing to be seen. The next day they questioned the antiques shop owner about the trunk, but he could offer no information regarding it. He added that he had experienced nothing of a supernatural nature while it had been with him. But the young couple took no chances — they threw the trunk on a bonfire as soon as they got home, and in so doing ridded themselves of the sinister, chuckling phantom.

Connah's Quay

Prolific writer of popular books on Welsh folklore, Jane Pugh, herself a resident of Connah's Quay on Deeside, has collected several accounts of a pack of spectral dogs said to haunt Wepre Park. The hounds are believed to emanate from "The Dogs' Graves," where generations of pets at Wepre Hall were buried, each with a little headstone.

Jane says that many older residents can remember mournful howlings and whines echoing through Wepre Woods, although the Hall's dogs were never let out after dark. A Shotton man out walking his dog one night was unnerved when his pet suddenly ran back to him along the path and cowered behind his legs. From around the corner came a pack of hounds silently running towards him. They were all of different shapes and sizes, but each appeared grey in the light of the moon.

They ignored him and his dog completely. About 100 yards from them they turned towards a path which leads to the Dogs' Graves, and at its entrance they vanished. An eerie howling then came from the graves' direction.

The hounds were seen under similar circumstances by a young couple in quite recent years.

Wepre is also haunted by the shade of a nun. Photographer Graham Catherall, a member of the angling club, told me the following story:

A few years ago an angler, late one summer night, saw a young boy running away from Wepre pool, apparently scared out of his wits. He stopped him and asked him what the matter was. The boy replied that he had seen "a horrible old nun" in the hedge, and that he had run away as fast as he could, leaving his gear behind.

Impressed firstly by the boy's obvious terror and secondly by the fact that he had abandoned his expensive fishing gear, the angler offered to accompany him back to the pool to investigate. There, the boy pointed out where he'd seen the nun. In the hedge the angler saw a dark shape receding, the leaves and twigs rustling even though it was a still evening.

Jane Pugh has recorded another account of the "nun" being seen at the pool, but dressed in white. It hovered into the air before a terrified young angler, and was shortly afterwards witnessed by two men standing by the shore.

Many years ago, states tradition (but not, apparently, historical fact), there stood at Wepre a convent, where one day a nun found a baby left on the doorstep. She carried it to Wepre Brook to wash it in the water — but it slipped from her grasp, and was washed downstream and drowned. The tragedy upset the nun deeply, and, eventually, unable to bear her shame, she returned to the brook, and forcing her face under the water, drowned herself. It is believed that it is her mournful spirit which haunts the pool.

Corwen

Lying in the vale of the River Dee, which meanders from Bala Lake (Llyn Tegid) through Llangollen to its estuary on Deeside, Corwen now seems somehow isolated, although it is still a thriving little town. It was once situated on one of the main routes through Wales to Holyhead on Anglesey (Ynys Môn) and therefore Ireland, and was also an important trading centre. A clue to its past importance are the many old hotels in its high street. The biggest of these, the Owain Glyndŵr, is reputedly haunted.

The story behind the haunting is a romantic one. A beautiful woman was once courted by a monk, but because of his vocation they had to keep their love a secret, and their meetings were clandestine. One day, however, their affair was discovered and the woman's brothers sent him away, leaving their sister waiting folornly for him forever. It is her sad ghost which is seen pacing the passages of the hotel, materialising frequently in a room called, unsurprisingly, "the haunted room."

A distressing experience befell a man in the centre of Corwen last century, when he suddenly found himself caught up in a phantom funeral. His account is quoted in noted folklorist Marie Trevelyan's 1909 book *Folklore and Folk Stories of Wales*:

"I was coming home late from a neighbouring village, when I suddenly heard wailing sounds a short distance ahead. I paused and listened, and suddenly found myself borne backwards in a funeral procession. I distinctly saw the coffin, and recognised one of the persons in the crowd beside me.

"With the procession I was borne onto the ancient parish church of St Julian, and not far from the doorway saw a well-known Dissenting minister approaching and joining us. Then the whole phantom vanished. I was greatly frightened and on reaching home promptly related my experiences.

"About fourteen days later a friend of ours died in Corwen. I went to the funeral and, arriving late, was pressed backward in the crowd. Near the old church, a well-known Dissenting minister joined the procession, and in it I recognised the people who had appeared previously as phantoms."

Spectres of funerals which act as a warning of a funeral to come are common in Welsh folklore, and we shall encounter another example at Ruabon near Wrexham.

Between Corwen and Cerrigydrudion, just off the A5 to Snowdonia, there is a deep, wooded chasm, through which surge the white waters of the Afon Ceirw. Seemingly inaccessible today, many hundred of years ago the valley was a much-used route to Ireland.

Its deeply wooded nature made the gorge an excellent place for ambush, and here many footpads and highwaymen lurked, ready to rob solitary travellers. It is said that so many murders have taken place in the valley that at night it is crammed with ghosts of robbers and travellers locked in memories of life or death combat.

Pont y Glyn, the little stone bridge spanning the gorge, now scarcely used, also has its ghost stories, of a varied nature. Shadowy figures, on horseback and on foot, have threatened many who have crossed it after sundown. On one occasion, according to Ken Radford in his *Tales of North Wales* (Skilton and Shaw 1982), a man threw himself under the horses of a coach from Cerrigydrudion, causing pandemonium. But when the road was searched for the shattered body, it was found to be empty.

Garthmeilio farm, at nearby Llangwm, is said to have been once haunted by a dairy maid murdered on the bridge by a jealous suitor.

By far the strangest of the ghosts encountered on Pont y Glyn was 'Ysbryd Ystrad Fawr', or Spirit of Ystrad Fawr farmhouse, which is at Llangwm. 'Ysbryd Ystrad Fawr' could make itself appear in many bizarre forms, including a huge turkey cock, or a red fire, or a big dog gnawing a bone.

It once appeared to a man in the guise of woman in traditional Welsh costume. The man bade the "woman" good evening but, without reply, the figure stood up and made its way off the bridge and down the road, swelling up like a balloon as it did so. By the time it had turned the corner and was out of sight the great wobbly mass was filling the thoroughfare!

Cwm

The elegant old hostelry of the Blue Lion at Cwm, near the coast, is the setting of one of Clwyd's best-authenticated ghost stories, that of John Henry, who lived in the 17th century, when the pub building was part of a farm. John owned the farm along with his father and brother. A quarrel broke out between them and it ended in John's murder. The next morning, father and son spread the news that John had emigrated to Australia, to cover up for his absence. In the 19th century, during a tidying up of the graveyard at the village church, which stands just behind the pub, a skeleton was found lying on top of a coffin — evidence of a very hasty burial. Many think that this was John's body.

John Henry has frequently been heard tramping the *Blue Lion's* corridors, and, in the 1960s at least, he was regularly seen, too. The wife of '60s landlord Stan Hughes would often encounter him. He would stand watching her for a few moments and then leave with a strange ducking motion of his head, as if he were passing under a now removed low doorway. He was once seen in the company of the ghosts of his father and brother.

John Henry would make his presence known in other ways, too. Mr Hughes kept a small menagerie behind the pub, but one morning in 1969 he found that all the animals — including a monkey, several snakes and an alligator — had been let out of their cages. He managed to round them up, but the same thing happened the next day. Suspecting the work of animal liberators, Mr Hughes sprinkled sand around the cages to secure impressions of the culprits' footprints. However, no footprints — other than those of the escaped animals — could be found in the sand the next morning. In all, this happened five times, even after stout wire had been wrapped round the padlocks.

The ghost has yet to appear to the present owners. Terry and Peggy Williams, but he has made himself known in other ways. Things are frequently falling off the walls for no apparent reason, especially if they are made of metal, such as horse brasses. One or more of the Williams' fascinating collection of antique chamber pots (200 in all), which decorates the ceiling, are often found unhooked and placed neatly on the

The Blue Lion, Cwm — stamping ground of the ghostly John Henry

floor. There is one room in the pub, noticeably colder than the rest, which the family dog avoids. She won't cross the threshold, even when called. This may be the site of John Henry's death.

It seems that John Henry is not the only ghost to haunt the *Blue Lion*. One day recently, the pub's cleaner passed the building and saw someone at the window of the private dining room upstairs. At first she assumed it was Mrs Williams, and waved. The figure remained motionless and then the cleaner realised that it was not Mrs Williams' face but that of an old woman. The pub, it later transpired, had been empty at the time. Possibly this was the same ghost as that seen by the young son of a previous owner some years ago. The boy was heard talking in his room late at night and he explained that he had been talking to a nice old lady in a blue dress, who had come in and lain down on the other bed, saying she wasn't feeling well. From a photograph, the boy later recognised the mysterious old woman as his grandmother, whom he had never met.

Cymau

To move into a haunted house may be thought unlucky — but to leave one only to move into another as equally haunted is surely very bad luck indeed! Such a misfortune befell the Butler family in 1886, when Mr Butler was appointed engineer to the Fron ironworks.

Their story is recorded by the Rev. Lee of Hanmer Church in his preacher's book (see Bronington). Mrs Butler, says the Rev. Lee, was left for a week to stay alone in Old Cymau Hall at the Ffrwd near Cymau. On the first night she was awoken by a tapping at the window.

A hollow voice called up to her from the darkness outside: "Pray for my soul!"

Mrs Butler hid under the covers, terrified, but the tapping continued and the voice repeatedly intoned its request. It went on all night, and Mrs

This hayloft is all that remains of New Cymau Hall — but according to its current owners still possesses an eerie atmosphere

Butler eventually fell into a fitfull sleep. She decided to say nothing of her experience the next morning.

But on the second night the insistent tapping came again at her window and again the voice moaned: "Pray for my soul!"

Mrs Butler tried to ignore the plea, but it was impossible. At last she managed a prayer, that the tortured soul, whosoever's it might be, should find rest. The tapping ceased and the voice was silenced. In the morning Mrs Butler told the housekeeper of the unearthly voice, and learnt that a man had killed himself quite recently outside the house, at a spot below her room.

A week later the Butlers moved — with some gratitude, I expect, from Mrs Butler — to New Cymau Hall, now Cymau Farm, on the slope of Hope Mountain. But every night, in their room above the drawing room, they found no rest.

Mr Butler was awoken by the feeling of someone putting a hand on his chest. Once, when Mrs Butler was alone, there was simultaneously a knocking at her door and at her mother's door. They both called out "Who is it?" and receiving no reply went to investigate, meeting each other, bemused, in the passageway.

According to the Rev. Lee, many people used the room in later years and suffered in just the way the Butlers did.

Denbigh

Denbigh, the county town of old Denbighshire, is built on a hill crowned by its fine castle, arguably the most impressive in the county. The town walls, contemporary with the castle, are equally as impressive and some of the best preserved of their kind in Europe. A few hundred yards below the castle, enshrouded in dark woods, is the Goblin Tower, an imposing edifice haunted by the ghost of the son of its Medieval builder, Henry de Lacy, the Earl of Lincoln. De Lacy had ordered the erection of the tower over a spring which supplied the castle with water. His son, a youth of fifteen, was playing on the scaffold of the half-built tower, when he lost his footing and fell to his death. The boy's face is said still to be seen, peering out of the black, socket-like windows. The castle itself is also said to have a ghost, one of the ubiquitous tribe of white ladies popular in Wales. She is said to walk the ramparts.

A white lady walks among the dramatic ruins of Denbigh Castle

A mysterious figure haunts the Book-Store in Vale Street. Proprietor Dot Roberts first noticed the presence while building work was being carried out at the shop in September 1989, prior to opening. She told me:

"I'd be working downstairs in the room over-looking the street and would often feel there was someone looking over my shoulder, but I didn't see anything for some time. Then, one morning, I walked into the room and there standing by the door was a young man in blue overalls, with long, greasy hair. He was looking at the floor and didn't move. Then he disappeared!

"I soon got used to having him around, because I'd see him most days. Then we bricked up a door, and opened up another, and that seemed to send him away. I thought he'd gone for good, but a few weeks later, I started seeing him again — but this time upstairs!

"I've seen him wandering around quite a lot now. I don't find him at all scary, he seems quite friendly. And the dog takes no notice of him either. But I haven't a clue who he might be."

The Goblin Tower looms among the dark woods which cloak Denbigh's impressive medieval town walls

Derwen

The charming, traditional stone-built village of Derwen, south of Ruthin, famous for the Dark Age ornamental cross in its churchyard, was once the scene of a rare sighting of a giant's ghost.

It was early one Mayday morning, and two youths were making their way home after performing an ancient custom called "fixing penglogau." It was the tradition on the night before Mayday for young men to fix tokens above the doors of the homes of the girls in the parish. If the young man felt favoured by a girl, he would attach a bouquet above her door, if rejected, a sheep's skull — penglogau. The two youths in this story must have been very unpopular with the local womenfolk because they had been out all night fixing the ghastly sheeps' skulls around the parish.

As they were approaching the bridge over the River Clwyd below Derwen, one of the youths suddenly saw descending the hillside before them a gigantic figure carrying a pine tree over his shoulder like a club. The boy stood in open-mouthed dismay as the giant began to cross over the bridge towards them. He watched as the giant heaved his pine tree into the river.

"What was that?" yelped his companion as there came an almighty splash. He had been unable to see the monstrous phantom, which, to the other boy's immense relief, had now completely vanished.

The ghost may have been that of one Sir John Salusbury, a giant of a man who lived in Denbigh in the 16th century. He was said to have eight fingers and two thumbs on each hand, and so was called 'Sir John of the Thumbs'. He used to pull grown pine trees out of the ground for exercise, and became famous for wrestling to death a lioness at Britain's first zoo, in the Tower of London, in the presence of Her Majesty Elizabeth I.

Efenechtyd

Apparitions have sometimes been wilfully created. *Yn rhamanta* is the name given to the practice by the Welsh to try and divine knowledge of future events. In general harmless, this divination was usually carried out by young people desirous to know who it was they were to marry.

At Efenechtyd, just south of Ruthin, a widow, Elizabeth Hughes, of Pentre Farm, hoped to be married again. Resorting to an old ritual to discover whether her hopes would be realised, she went with a serving girl to a pistyll, or natural water spout. There, repeating some lines now lost to history, she washed one of her garments, beating it repeatedly with a mallet, and invoked the presence of her future husband to appear.

Suddenly, the mallet was taken from her. A man she knew had appeared at her side. Without a word he continued to beat the linen just as she had done. Greatly frightened, widow Hughes ran home to her farm. It soon came to pass that she did marry the man whose apparition had come to her that day, despite considerable opposition from her children.

At nearby Cyffylliog two young women practised *rhamanta* to see their future husbands — and did so. Kitty Jones and another servant at Plas Nant farm let their mistress know that on two successive midnights each would be attempting "to lift the veil of the future."

On the first night, as the clock chimed 12, Kitty's fellow-servant began to strike the floor with a leather strap, repeating the magic lines. As she did so, her master came down the stairs. The next day the girl innocently asked her mistress why she had sent her master down to frighten her, but her mistress's only reply was: "Take care of my children." And in the end, that girl did marry her master.

The following midnight it was Kitty's turn to perform the ritual. She saw a dark man she had never seen before. However, a week or two later, the same man came into the farmyard. She inquired after him and discovered that he was a Mr Jones, and, to her dismay, that he was married. However, not long after, his wife died, and so Kitty became Kitty Jones.

Ewloe

The atmospheric ruins of Ewloe Castle are in a very unusual setting. Rather than being built, as most fortresses are, on some hill or other prominence, the castle lies in a hollow — in the middle of a wood. The castle was built in the 12th century by the celebrated Welsh prince, Llywelyn ap Gwynedd, to replace a Norman manor house. Many strange happenings have been experienced here; the castle walls seem resonant with psychic activity.

A recent custodian of the castle would regularly hear the sound of singing emanating from the ramparts, particularly during thunderstorms. One evening he went to investigate and saw a glowing white figure standing high on one of the ruined towers. He later saw the same apparition pass through a hedge, and on another occasion it frightened a

Ewloe Castle, scene of a fascinating variety of supernatural phenomena

dog so badly that it died two days later. The vet could find nothing physically wrong with the animal, and put the fatality down to shock.

Phantom lights have also been reported, playing around the walls and towers. More than one witness has also heard the sound of marching men, tramping through the woods approaching the castle, but never arriving.

Flint

A bus depot may seem a strange place for a haunting, but according to Jane Pugh in her *Welsh Ghostly Encounters* (Gwasg Carreg Gwalch, 1990), Flint's has two.

Late one night two employees were getting ready to go home when they noticed the figure of a girl in a long dress with a shawl over her head loitering around the back of the depot. She was shortly joined by another, indistinct figure. The two men went to investigate, but were startled when the figures "seemed to spiral off the ground and disappear."

For two hundred years apparitions have been reported in the area where the bus depot was built. It is said they are the spirits of two tragic lovers, united by suicide.

Opposite the depot is the site of Flint Manor Farm. In the 18th century a 16-year-old girl, daughter of the squire of Flint Manor (now demolished), fell in love with a labourer of Flint Manor Farm, and secretly they planned to marry. But the girl's father discovered the affair, and warned the tenant of the farm that if he did not have the youth removed from service and sent away, he would lose his tenancy.

The squire locked his daughter in her room, but she escaped to warn her lover of the plan to have him removed. They agreed to elope.

Having second thoughts, however, the youth decided he could not allow the girl to give up her comfortable life and suffer the hardship of a life on the road with him, so, that morning, he left without her. When the girl discovered this, and that she would not see her love again, she took a knife and plunged it into her heart, killing herself instantly. Her maid found her lying in her blood-soaked bed the following morning.

A week later, however, the boy returned to the farm. He had been unable to face a life alone, and crept in for one last talk with his love. He soon learnt of the tragedy. With a cry of despair, he ran into one of the barns, and there hanged himself.

His angry, restless spirit soon began to haunt the barn, and the farmyard. A priest was called in to exorcise it but only succeeded in transferring its presence to the manor grounds. Not long after, the spirit of his bride joined him, and, it is said, they have haunted the area ever since.

Jane Pugh also describes a dip in the road between Flint and Connah's Quay which appears to possess a destructive presence which loathes road-users. Many motorists have felt invisible hands tugging at their wheel, nearly forcing them off the road with fatal consequences, and cyclists have experienced similar interference. Even pedestrians have felt themselves possessed with a sudden, dangerous compulsion to walk out into the middle of the road despite the busy traffic.

The dip, named Edmund's Hollow, possibly after a former excise officer, is said to be the site where a drowned dairymaid called Mary was hauled ashore; allegedly the inspiration for Charles Kingsley's famous poem "Mary call the cattle home across the sands o' Dee." Perhaps it is her spirit which so harrasses users of the road.

Glyn Ceiriog

Glyn Ceiriog is enviably situated amongst some of the most beautiful scenery in Clwyd, the breathtaking Ceiriog valley. Glyn Ceiriog was the birthplace, in 1700, of John Edwards, bookseller, poet and — if tradition is to be believed — magician. Among Edwards' more orthodox achievements were the composition of an ode to Llangollen and the translating into Welsh of Bunyan's *Pilgrim's Progress*. The locals, however, avoided his door, suspicious of a man with so much learning, and were convinced that he had dealings with the black arts, and communed with spirits. Ghosts, they said, were at his beck and call, and he used them like servants. Every morning a phantom would carry him into the air from his remote home over the steep glen, so he could make his way to the village in safety! Whatever the truth of these tales, Edwards was certainly an eccentric and apparently endowed with a dubious sense of humour — he named his sons Cain and Abel!

According to a little book, written and published by Michael Bartlett in Wirral, *Britain's Most Haunted Places*, which was kindly lent to me by Owen Elias of Rhostyllen, a nearby quarry is the scene of a haunting. In 1872, a workman at Hendre Quarry stole a mate's wages. He was soon discovered and pursued by his outraged fellows, right to the edge of the quarry. The thief lost his footing and slipped — and fell screaming to his death. To this day, says Mr Bartlett, bloodcurdling screams are still to be heard echoing round the cliffs.

Gresford

For most the prospect of seeing a ghost is a frightening one. It is common, however, for a witness to meet a ghost and be totally unaware of the fact. Passing someone in an unfamiliar house, automatically saying hello, but then, on realising that the person was wearing old-fashioned clothes, turning to find he has vanished — that is the typical pattern.

But how much more frightening, how much more horrible, to see the ghost of someone one has known, perhaps unaware that that person is even dead. Sometimes a person's image can be projected at the moment of death. Such an image is known as a "crisis apparition."

A particularly distressing example of a crisis apparition was encountered on the road between the villages of Gresford and Marford, near Wrexham, in the 19th century. Two men, William Davies, a builder from Marford, and his friend Mr Williams, who lived at the Old Parsonage in Gresford, were out one evening taking a stroll. As they reached the bottom of Little Acton Hill near the old Blue Bell pub they saw approaching them a woman dressed all in white.

Peering through the gathering gloom, the men recognised the woman as Mr Williams' wife. As it was rather late they imagined that perhaps she had come in search of her wayward husband.

"Now you're for it!" joked Mr Davies.

But Mrs Williams said nothing as she came upon them. She seemed hardly aware of the two men, and there was a wild expression on her pale face. Suddenly, she was no longer there! Dumbstruck, the two friends searched for her, but she was nowhere to be seen. Finally, reluctantly, they continued on their way, talking about what they had seen.

They tried to rationalise the extraordinary event. Mr Williams could only imagine that his wife had played some kind of practical joke on him, but he was feeling increasingly uneasy. By the time the men reached the turn where their paths diverged, he was feeling quite anxious. Bidding his friend goodnight, Mr Williams hurried home.

He found the Old Parsonage in darkness and as silent as the grave. Fumbling for his key, he let himself in. The kitchen was empty and nothing had been left for his supper. He called out for his wife, but no answer came. Nervously he lit a candle and systematically began to search the house. He found his wife in the sitting room — she was hanging from the neck, a suicide.

Gwernymynydd

One evening (in 1990) I spoke to a friend, Matthew Johnson, regarding a ghost he had seen in his home, Tŷ Gwernen, Gwernymynydd, on the shallow hills overlooking Mold. A few years ago he had been lying in bed, recovering from a back injury, when he saw the face of an old woman staring in at him through the window.

"It was the most horrible face I have ever seen," said Matthew, "very wrinkled, ugly, and, in my frightened state, it also looked very evil. It glared at me for a few moments and then vanished."

A few hours after I was told this story, a strange coincidence took place. Just after midnight I received an unexpected 'phone call from an excited Matthew:

"You're not going to believe this," he said, "but I've just got home to find there's been another sighting!"

The witness, Matthew's younger brother, Edward, aged 14, was then put on to me. Clearly still shaken by the experience, he told me:

"I was on my own in the house watching television in the sitting room when suddenly this old woman walked into the room. She was very old and white haired, with a thin face. She walked into the middle of the room and stood in front of the fire, staring at the wall. It was terrifying, she was just a few feet in front of me. But she didn't seem to be aware of me at all. After a few moments she slowly disappeared. I've spent the rest of the night hiding in the kitchen!"

Edward then recalled a previous unsettling occasion in another room, when the family cats suddenly took exception to something unseen (by him) in the room. As one they all turned to stare at the sofa and then, hissing furiously, ran out with their fur bristling.

Eldest brother Daniel, 21, frequently hears unexplained tappings and scratches in his bedroom on the first floor, but as yet he hasn't seen the ghost and neither have the boys' parents, Dave and Ann Johnson.

There is a story attached to the house which may explain the apparition. It is said that about a hundred years ago (the date is uncertain) an old woman lived in the house with a mentally handicapped son. Attitudes being what they were in the past, particularly in rural areas, the son was a

*Matthew and Edward Johnson outside their haunted home,
Tŷ Gwernen, Gwernymynydd*

*Daniel Johnson walks the gloomy lane at Gwernymynydd where he
encountered a giant, shadow-like phantom*

source of shame to the woman and she kept him locked in the house out of sight. The resulting tension finally broke, and in a rage the son murdered his mother, possibly by strangling her.

The ghost of Tŷ Gwernen is not the only supernatural presence in the area, for the quiet road leading from Gwernymynydd village up to Tŷ Gwernen is also haunted, and Daniel Johnson is one of those who has seen the apparition. He told me:

"I had been walking home up the road leading from the Swan Inn, just before dusk, when I saw in front of me this huge shape, a silhouette about seven feet tall, completely featureless, just solid black. It was about twenty yards in front of me and staggering about the road, from side to side, like it was drunk! It was a sort of oblong shape, as if whoever it was was wearing a long, heavy overcoat.

"I was really scared, to be honest, but what could I do? It was between me and home! I just slowed my speed a bit and watched it as it lurched its way up the road.

"I think if it had turned round, I'd have run for it, but, thankfully, it just continued on its way, until, opposite one of the roadside houses, it vanished. I don't know what it was, but I know I don't want to see it again!"

Halkyn

Halkyn Mountain can seem a mournful place. The lead that was once dragged from beneath it during earlier days of frantic mining activity has poisoned the soil, so that in parts only thin, yellowish grass will grow and the only living creatures to be seen are a few near-wild sheep and the occasional crow.

Away from the small, select communities which line the hill, commanding views across the wide, blue Dee estuary to Wirral, Halkyn Mountain has a desolate air, silent and lonely.

It is indeed the place for a ghost, and one has frequently been seen wandering along one of the numerous narrow, winding roads that traverse it. Many going to work along the road, which connects the villages of Pentre Halkyn and Milwr, have come across him, walking ahead, head down, carrying a large bag under his arm.

The *Flintshire Leader* investigated the sightings in 1970, and found many witnesses. A Mr John Rees of Pentre Halkyn was quoted as saying:

"I've seen whispy figures in the road dozens of times but one particular morning we saw something that really startled us. There was a man wearing a short coat and carrying a bag under his arm. It was a nasty morning so we stopped to pick him up. We had the fright of our lives when he just disappeared."

A friend, Mr William Lloyd, described the ghost as: " . . . a misty figure — bluish grey in colour — and it zig-zagged its way up the road and vanished through a gap in the hedge."

Mr Lloyd claimed to have seen the figure on three separate occasions whilst travelling to work.

It has also been seen in the evening. A Mr Gordon Davies of Pentre Halkyn reported his encounter:

"I was going out with friends one evening when I saw what looked like an ordinary man wearing a raincoat walking along the road. I braked hard because I thought I would hit him, but the figure just disappeared. It wasn't my imagination, because we all saw it."

The *Leader* reporter went in search of the ghost himself several times at night and on one occasion thought he saw a figure run across the road

A murdered man still walks this winding road on Halkyn Mountain

before him. To explain the ghost he puts forward the story that a medieval court was had at one of the old lead mines nearby and an innocent man was hanged there.

Rather more likely than this local legend is the story that a man whose job it was to deliver pay to miners employed around the mountain during the 19th century was murdered for the cash he carried as he made his way up the lane, and now haunts the scene of his violent death.

Hawarden

Hawarden, near Chester, is famous for once being the home of Gladstone, four-times Prime Minister during the reign of Victoria. His shade has often been seen wandering around the 'Castle', his former residence, and also St Deiniol's Library, a residential library with a superb collection of works on theology. Gladstone was himself devoutly religious and a great classical scholar.

It was here, a few years ago, that he was seen by poet Gladys Mary Coles, who had taken a residency at the library.

"I didn't realise he was a ghost at first," Gladys Mary told me. "He was sitting on a seat by a big, bright window, reading a book. I smiled in his direction as I came past him on the staircase, and wondered who he was, since I'd not seen him in St Deiniol's before. He seemed so absorbed in his book that I felt too shy to say hello.

"Then, as I began to descend the stairs, it occurred to me what very old-fashioned clothes he'd beeen wearing, and I looked back — and there he was, gone! I realised then that it was a ghost I'd seen and, strangely, it didn't really frighten me, just made me feel curious. There were enough paintings of Gladstone around on the walls for me to soon discover who it was I'd seen.

"I later spoke to a porter in the library, who told me that the seat where I'd seen Gladstone was a favourite of his because the light from the window allowed him to read for longer, and others had seen his ghost there, too."

Before it was enlarged and given its castellated appearance, Gladstone's former home was named Broadlane and was a pretty, black and white Tudor manor house. Here, in the early years of the 18th century, lived the Glynne family, who harboured an ancient hatred for the Cratchleys of nearby Deiniol's Ash Manor House, standing by the road to Mancot.

In true Romeo and Juliet fashion, a son of the Glynne family, William, fell in love with a daughter of the Cratchley's, Rebecca. They kept their meetings clandestine, because of the enmity between the two houses, but eventually they were found out, with tragic consequences. William's furious father had his son packed off to Europe on a Grand Tour in the hope he would forget his attachment, but in France, at Aix la Chapelle, in 1730, he died, leaving a heartbroken Rebecca to pine folornly for him forever.

Rebecca's sad ghost haunted Deiniol's Ash, now called Ash Farm, for many years after. In 1935 she was seen by D . . . E . . . , then a young girl living in Mancot. She and a few friends were making their way to a New Year's Eve dance at the old Hawarden Gym. It was 7 o'clock.

D . . . said: "As we we were walking towards Ash Farm, a figure came towards us from the small gateway and continued to walk into the road, where it disappeared. We dropped our things and ran! We then met up with a man called G . . . W . . . who asked us to go back with him after telling him the story, but we refused to go past, so he went back to pick up our things for us!"

At the small airfield near Hawarden the figure of a World War 2 RAF sergeant has been seen. He stands near where a fighter plane crashed in a ball of flames in 1941, and so may be the spirit of its doomed pilot.

The Glynne Arms by the cross in Hawarden is reputed to be haunted. Guy Lion Playfair in his "Haunted Pub Guide" (Harrap Ltd, 1985) says that the sound of feminine feet has been heard pattering down an upstairs corridor, pausing by a bedroom door, upon which light taps are heard. A former landlord, he states, also experienced a phantom smell, "rather like some kind of perfume."

When I spoke to landlord Mr A. Withington in 1987, he admitted he'd never encountered these manifestations; but he could offer another ghost story about his elegant inn.

"A boy of 12 is supposed to have been killed outside when a horse bolted," said Mr Withington. "He was carried through the double doors at the front and died in the corridor. Now his ghost is supposed to haunt the place."

Henllan

Many are the inns of Britain which claim a ghost. One of the oldest and most attractive is the *Llindir* at Henllan near Denbigh. The ghost of this thatched 13th century hostelry, which is overshadowed by the curious, detached bell tower of the church, perched on an outcrop high above the village, bears the name of Sylvia and she dates back 300 years to when the inn was owned by a sea captain.

During the long months when her husband was at sea, Sylvia would regularly forget her vows of fidelity and would sport in the marriage bed with many of the local young bloods. On one fateful, stormy night, however, she was found out. Her husband returned home unexpectedly. Caught in the storm, wet-through and not in the best of moods, he headed straight for his bedchamber after some dry clothes and a warm welcome from his wife. But as he stumbled into the room the only warmth he felt was one of hot fury, for he found there Sylvia busy engaged with her latest amour.

Enraged beyond reason, he leapt on the bed, drew his dagger and stabbed his wife's lover through the heart. As a terrified Sylvia desperately begged forgiveness for her betrayal, her husband's hands closed slowly round her throat, and her excuses were choked off as he strangled her to death.

Sylvia's sad spirit, dressed in a long gown of blue, has since haunted the *Llindir*, though she has been seen less and less frequently in recent years. Even after death, it seems Sylvia did not give up her amorous ways. It was said that if any man slept alone in the room where Sylvia died, her ghost would creep into bed with him! BBC reporters Fyfe Robertson and Cliff Michelmore once stayed in the inn to test this tradition — but were disappointed (or perhaps relieved!) when she failed to materialise.

Echoes of the murder have also possibly remained at the inn, frightening the living. In 1960, a holidaymaker staying in the "haunted bedroom" woke up shivering, and felt hands around his throat. The sheets and blankets were pulled from his bed and he heard noises of a struggle. A member of an amateur psychic investigation team researching the phenomena claimed to have been pushed out of bed by an unseen presence, and an ex-seaman called "Old Pop", who lived in at the pub, said that he was once pushed downstairs by the ghost.

It is possible that it is not only the hapless Sylvia but also her murderous husband who haunts the *Llindir*.

Holt

If at midnight you should cross over the Medieval sandstone bridge spanning the River Dee on the Welsh/English border at Holt, steel yourself should you hear the chilling sound of children screaming as they drown in the black water swirling below.

During the reign of Edward I the bridge was the scene of a cowardly murder. Madog ap Gruffudd of Dinas Brân, Llangollen, had died, leaving two sons, aged eight and ten, with no trustees. The king placed their guardianship in the hands of John, Earl Warren, and Roger Mortimer of Wigmore. But the cruel lords plotted to rid themselves of this burden and to gain for themselves the wealth the boys would receive on their coming of age.

One night the lords took the boys on horseback from Chester to Dinas Brân, and, as they crossed the bridge by the (now demolished) Lady's Chapel, they halted and gently took down from their mounts their sleeping wards. Then, as one they heaved the helpless boys over the parapets and into the freezing waters of the river beneath. The boys screamed in terror, begging for rescue as their clothes dragged them relentlessly down, but Warren and Mortimer stood and watched and waited until they were drowned, smiling with satisfaction the while.

It is said those pitiful cries are still heard at dead of night echoing from beneath the bridge so that the cruel deed should not be forgotten.

It is possible this murder had royal approval, and had been intended by the king from the start when he appointed the evil lords as guardians. For, rather than being punished, the lords, in fact, attained some of the boys' estates for themselves — the rest, presumably, being claimed by the Crown.

Holywell

A haunting which has been recounted in several books is that of the *Talacre Arms* public house at Holywell, a few hundred yards up the hill from the famous St Winifred's Well, once known as the 'Lourdes of Wales' because of its healing properties.

Most of the phenomena attributed to the haunting were copied from a news report from the late seventies — which was unfortunately rather exaggerated in its account. Of the most dramatic phenomena described, and repeated in several books, were inexplicable beer glass filling, lightbulbs coming out of their sockets and remaining alight, and the piano playing on its own. It was also stated that landlord Mark Sumner and a dozen customers watched a picture mysteriously swinging backwards and forwards on the wall.

In fact, none of these things took place, and Mark Sumner told me that it was slightly embarrassing to keep reading that they had. However, some inexplicable phenomena have occurred at the Talacre, and there is some basis for the wild claims quoted above.

For example, one morning several bottles above the bar were found to be missing — although the frames that they had been in, and the optics they had been attached to, were still there. A full measure of spirit was left in each optic and there was no sign of any spillage on the floor or surfaces below. It was demonstrated to me how an attempt to remove an upturned bottle from an optic without some of its contents pouring out was impossible — without turning it the right way up again, in which case the optic would drain back out.

The large sliding door to the bar, locked and bolted the previous night, was standing open, but although these odd few bottles were missing, loose bottles, much easier to steal, and many packets of cigarettes kept behind the bar, were untouched.

The spirit with a taste for spirits did also have a penchant for light bulbs, causing several to fall from their sockets for no apparent reason, but none remained alight while they did so. One evening a bulb in a newly-fitted screw-in socket fell onto the pool table, extremely hot. It was removed and another fitted. Five minutes later this too fell from the screw-in socket, also very hot. A third was fitted — and promptly exploded. A local, John James, said he found this particularly unnerving because it only seemed to happen when it was his turn to take a shot!

Animals are especially sensitive to the presence. A labrador leapt straight through a window in obvious terror from something unseen by the family, and another dog suddenly yelped and bolted away into the road, and was killed by a car. They have tried to keep several dogs at the pub, but none would settle, and many just disappeared. One puppy would attempt to escape whenever it saw an open door. After alterations had been carried out at the pub, this dog began to howl in the night. One evening, the howling being particularly persistent, Mark investigated, opening the door of the cellar where it was kept, and was startled to find the light on, the lower door to the room wide open and the puppy cowering in a corner.

Contrary to this apparent animosity directed towards pets, however, a saucer of meat was found placed invitingly on the floor of a locked upstairs room, presumably left there by the ghost, for no-one had been in the room since the morning. The saucer was unlike any other in the house, as a root through all the cupboards substantiated, and a check with the neighbours showed it unlikely to have come from the immediate surroundings. The origin of the meat was also a mystery. Possibly it was left for a cat; a regular, Alan Davies, and a friend, once felt something cat-like, but invisible, brush the back of their legs while they were standing at the bar.

The hauntings at the Talacre remain enigmatic; there is no story to account for them. But the presence continues to make itself quietly known, footsteps occasionally being heard, previously shut doors found inexplicably open, and objects disappearing without trace, only to turn up where they went missing a few days later.

Hope

Halfway between the villages of Hope and Higher Kinnerton, beside the road to Shordley Manor, there stands a large, rough-hewn stone. Now unmarked, the stone once bore a crudely chiselled cross. It is the wayside grave of two brothers, brought to an untimely end by greed and jealousy.

Living at a nearby farmhouse, the brothers were sons of an aged farmer who was close to death. Both sons stood to gain the inheritance, but neither wished the other to get it, and there was envy and malice between them. One night, one of the brothers waylaid the other at the spot where now stands the stone and murdered him. He was buried where he lay and the stone erected over him.

However, it was not long before the guilty brother was found out, and he was hanged for the murder. His body was buried alongside that of his brother beneath the stone. And now, it is said, if you pass that way at dead of night you will see the wraiths of the two brothers locked in silent, deadly combat.

Mr James Bentley, Buckley historian, recorded this tale for the Clwyd Oral History Library. He added: "I used to pass that spot on my bike on many occasions, at the dead of night. I never saw any ghost — I was peddling too fast — but I did feel an icy atmosphere."

Llanasa

Thyme is a herb which features strongly in British folklore. It is closely associated with death, possibly because it was an important ingredient in ancient embalming processes. In the parish of Llanasa, between the village and Mostyn, a hundred years ago, stood the ruins of a pair of old cottages called Yr-ardd-ddu. The distinct smell of thyme could often be smelt by passers-by on the road outside these cottages, although no thyme had grown there for many years.

Centuries ago, a foul murder took place at one of these cottages. Two small children were killed by their guardian and buried in the garden. Their bodies were covered over with a bed of thyme.

Since then the ghosts of the children were said to haunt the place, and the scent of thyme remained as an echo to remind future generations of the evil deed.

Llanddulas

On the coast at Llanddulas, which, tradition tells us, was once the home of the Devil — he lived in a cave in the cliffs above the village — there is a sturdy, stone-built house named Pendyffryn. In the 19th century, Pendyffryn was the residence of Sir Alfred Lewis Jones KCMG, a Liverpool Shipping magnate who opened up trade links with West Africa, developed the banana trade and also, in 1899, founded the Liverpool School of Tropical Medicine.

Today it is the haunt of a peaceful lady ghost, who has appeared from time to time over the last 20 years. She always appears in the same part of the house at the same time of day, and is not in the least bit frightening to the present residents. She is believed to be the ghost of an elderly housekeeper and she usually manifests herself after alterations or building work has taken place at the hall.

Llandegla

Llandegla was the site of another exorcism by the celebrated Rev. Griffiths. A poltergeist had set up home in the Rectory, annoying the residents and throwing utensils around the kitchen, stones around the ground and clods of earth at passers-by on the road outside.

Rev. Griffiths performed his usual method of chalking two circles on the floor, standing in one himself and commanding the spirit to appear in the other. It did so, and in many frightful forms, but eventually Rev. Griffiths succeeded in compelling it into the shape of a small fly. This he imprisoned, and buried under a large stone in the river beneath a bridge near the old Llandegla Mills. He charged the spirit to remain there until a sapling growing on the river bank reached the height of the bridge's parapet.

For many years after, the village children would trim the branches of this tree so that it would never reach the critical height, but this custom was abandoned in the 19th century and the tree now stands taller than the bridge — and we must assume the spirit has escaped to wreak havoc elsewhere!

A violent ghost once haunted the Mold road between Llandegla and Rhydtalog, at a spot called Boncyn y Porthman, or 'the Drover's Bank'. A drover was murdered here by robbers in the 18th century. It was said the unfortunate man's wraith could be seen hovering mistlike above the hedges near where he was killed.

Waggoners would experience considerable difficulty in guiding their horses past this spot, for terror would come upon them as they approached. A darkness would come over the place, a high wind would rise, and the horses, sweating with fear, would try to back away.

One night, a farmer was returning late from Chester market, when he saw a man approach him from the bank. The man, whose features were indistinct, dragged from his horse and without a word proceeded to beat him up, leaving go only when the unfortunate man was unconscious.

The next morning, when the farmer awoke, battered and bruised he was astonished to discover that he had not been robbed. So perplexed was he by this unprovoked assault that he could only conclude that it was the ghost that had attacked him.

In 1890, workmen on the road discovered a Bronze Age burial at Drover's Bank. Perhaps it was some ancient and primitive spirit that haunted the site, guarding the grave.

Llangernyw

Every Hallowe'en a spirit called Angelystor (or the "Recording Angel") would manifest itself at Llangernyw church at midnight and solemnly intone the names of those in the parish who were to die during the coming year.

Not everyone in the village believed in the existence of Angelystor, however. Particularly sceptical was a tailor, Siôn Robert. One Hallowe'en night, after he had quaffed an especially generous quantity of *cwrw da* ('good ale'), Siôn announced loudly in his local inn that he was going to the church to prove that Angelystor was a myth.

His fellow drinkers urged to him to change his mind and not to tempt fate, but, scoffing at their superstitious fear, Siôn swept dramatically out of the pub and headed for the church. There he could faintly discern a voice coming from behind the church door. Cautiously Siôn opened the door a crack and then heard the name "Siôn Robert!" called from within.

"Wait!" cried Siôn. "I am not ready!" But ready or not, Siôn Robert the tailor died that very year . . .

In the autumn of 1891 two young people stumbled upon the scene of an ancient and bloody battle, re-enacted invisibly around them. They had been returning from the fair at Llanrwst, when, near a lake called Chwythlyn, south-west of Llangernyw, they became lost in a thick fog which suddenly descended upon them. They took shelter in a wood by the lake's shore, and huddled together among the dripping pine trees to keep warm.

The silence was broken by a sound like the sighing of the wind. The sound grew steadily louder and then became distinguishable as the sounds of battle. Soon it seemed as if fierce fighting was going on all around the frightened couple. Men's screams, the clash of weapons, the rumble of chariot wheels and the regular thump-thump of wardrums echoed among the trees, but the mist obscured all sight of the antagonists. This went on for more than an hour, and then the noises subsided, the mist lifted and the youngsters found themselves alone in the moonlit wood. Shivering with shock and cold, they escaped the wood and made their way home.

A few months later the bodies of the young couple were found floating face down in the freezing water of the lake. They had seemed happy to their friends and neighbours, and there was no suggestion of a suicide, so the deaths were completely inexplicable. Had their experience so disturbed them that they were compelled to take their own lives, or did an even more terrifying encounter by the lake lead to their deaths? The mystery was never solved.

The area around Chwythlyn has yielded many Roman artefacts over the years, weapons included. Perhaps it was the echo of a battle fought thousands of years ago that the youngsters heard, an affray between Romans and Celtic warriors defending their land from invasion.

Llangollen

In 1779, two very remarkable characters came to live in the heart of the glorious Vale of Llangollen.

Lady Eleanor Butler and Miss Sarah Ponsonby ran away together from their native Ireland and journeyed through the Welsh interior, pausing at Llangollen, where they fell in love with one especially beautiful view from a peasant's cottage. Here they were discovered by Miss Ponsonby's family, and she was taken back to Ireland. But the couple vowed that when Sarah came of age they would live together at the spot they had discovered; and did so, buying the humble cottage from the peasant with a bag of gold, and building in its place Plas Newydd, a fine mock Tudor mansion.

Lady Butler and Miss Ponsonby lived at Plas Newydd until their deaths in the early 1800s, rarely going abroad beyond its grounds. They cut their hair short and wore men's clothes, and, as 'The Ladies of Llangollen', became famous as cultured eccentrics. Wordsworth, Sir Walter Scott, the Duke of Wellington, and members of royal houses across Europe were among the many important guests of the Ladies of Llangollen.

It is no wonder that such forceful characters should continue to roam the house they built and loved for so many years as ghosts, and their mannish figures have occasionally been seen strolling round the grounds.

Another famous figure of the past who has been said to have made his presence known again in Llangollen is none other than Owain Glyndŵr, the hero of the Welsh people. Owain was declared a traitor by Henry IV after a cruel deception by a grasping English lord with designs on his land. Owain rebelled and thousands joined his fight against English supremacy. Eventually, in 1410, his armies were defeated, and Owain disappeared. The date or location of his death have never been verified by historians.

Owain's spirit is said to have materialised at a number of places around Wales. He once made an appearance at Valle Crucis Abbey, now no more than a romantic ruin by the side of the road leading into town. The Abbot was enjoying a stroll one evening when from out of nowhere a man in warrior's garb approached him. The Abbot knew instinctively that this was Owain Glyndŵr's spirit, and he struck up conversation. Owain told him that one day England would be ruled by monarchs of Welsh descent. The Abbot later spread this prophesy abroad — and it proved true when the Tudors took the throne (see Llannefydd).

Valle Crucis was the scene of another apparition — more a vision — seen in recent years by a Wrexham woman. In a letter she described her experience to me:

"Walking one night on the road opposite Valle Crucis with my aunt, we stopped to peer through the darkness to the Abbey. I was annoyed to see in front of the Abbey the ground suddenly light up in a large circle of the most dazzling light — apparently emanating from the ground. In the middle of the circle there was some kind of golden object, several feet high, and walking about quite a number of human figures, garbed in wonderful golden costumes with golden kind of helmets on their heads.

"I had never seen such a radiant scene. I said to my aunt: 'Isn't it wonderful — everything in that shining, golden light. It must be some kind of pageant they are putting on.' I couldn't believe it when she replied: 'What light? What pageant? It's all dark.' In some seconds the wonderful scene went on, but she couldn't see it. Then suddenly it finished as suddenly as it had come."

It is possible this vision was the apparition of some elaborate Pagan or early Christian ceremony held on the Abbey site hundreds of years ago. The "golden light" may have been no more than the ghost of daylight. The ghosts most often said to be encountered at Valle Crucis are much more drab in comparison; phantom monks in brown habits, sometimes in procession.

According to Peter Underwood in his *Ghosts of Wales* (Christopher Davies, 1978), there is one more haunting in Llangollen, that of a young woman who haunts a fisherman's cottage beside the River Dee. She is a quiet presence, but often seen by the owners, and by visitors. Who she is, and why she haunts the building, however, is unknown.

Llangynhafal

Plas Draw, an old oak-panelled house near Llangynhafal in the Vale of Clwyd, has several ghosts and also an amusing tale told about it.

In the reign of George III, the squire of the house was a nervous old miser, possessed of a considerable treasure of family silver. This he kept hidden away in a secret compartment in the seat of a specially constructed armchair, where he would sit all day with much peace of mind.

One day a servant of his went to seek his fortune in London. He didn't find it, but instead fell in with a company of housebreakers. He told this team of ruffians of the valuables he knew were stored away, he knew not where, in the house of his former employment. Encouraged by Plas Draw's isolated position, the gang journeyed up to Wales to rob the old man.

A Georgian facade hides the much older, timber-framed structure of Plas Draw at Llangynhafal

They searched the house from top to bottom, but could not find the silver. To keep the terrified squire still, they bound him to his chair, and tried to force him to reveal the location of his treasure. But the squire remained tight-lipped — sitting on it all throughout the interrogation!

Eventually, the villains gave up and left, but not before a small boy, the son of one of the housemaids, had witnessed the robbery through a window and had raised the alarm. The would-be thieves were pursued over Bwlch Penbarras, the pass over the mountains, and eventually caught. The unfortunate ex-servant was hanged at Denbigh.

And it is his sad-faced ghost which is said to haunt the hall, still searching for the treasure which eluded him. Other ghostly phenomena have also been experienced here. A piano has been heard playing in an unoccupied room and an electrician working alone in another room was suddenly so overcome by a sense of evil that he upped and fled, leaving behind his tools and flatly refusing to return for them!

Llannefydd

One of Clwyd's most historic houses is the old manor of Berain at Llannefydd. Here, in the 16th century, lived Catrin Tudor, a kinswoman of the then monarch, Elizabeth I. Catrin had so many noble descendents that she earned the name Mam Cymru, or the 'Mother of Wales'.

According to legend, however, this cosy nickname belies an evil, scheming personality. Catrin, says tradition, had seven husbands (she actually had four), and she murdered all of them — by pouring molten lead into their ears! She buried each of her unfortunate spouses in the orchard at dead of night. The orchard has a correspondingly eerie reputation, with old tales of unearthly screams heard at dead of night and misty figures seen drifting between the trees.

On one occasion, an attempt to murder one of her husbands by the

Berain, Llannefydd — home of the cruel Mam Cymru

convenient lead method became rather messy when he woke up — and Catrin was forced to improvise with a large knife. She stabbed the unfortunate man over and over, until finally he gorily expired. The legacy of this horrible incident is an indelible bloodstain on the panelling, which would reappear never mind how often it was washed off.

The ghost of a woman in Elizabethan costume is also reputed to haunt the hall, and is presumed to be Catrin herself. She is seen with head bowed, clasping and unclasping her hands, and uttering belated moans of remorse. No doubt she has good reason to feel sorry for herself, with seven vengeful ghosts patrolling the grounds outside!

Llanrhaeadr-yng-Nghinmeirch

The little village of Llanrhaeadr-yng-Nghinmeirch near Denbigh has a lovely stone church blessed with a rare and beautiful Jesse Window, depicting in medieval stained glass Christ's family tree. In the churchyard, in the latter years of the 18th century, the body of Ann Parry, an early methodist preacher who set up a Sunday School in the village, was buried. Forty-three years later, when her tomb was opened to admit the body of her son, Ann Parry's body was found to still be in a perfect state of preservation. The corpse, according to Sabine Baring-Gould in *A Book of North Wales* (1903), was found to be "undecayed in the slightest degree and her countenance bearing the hues of living health."

The author continues: "The very flowers which had been strewed upon the body, it is said, were as fresh in colour and as fragrant in odour as when

The wicked Dafydd Salusbury rides for all eternity round the churchyard at Llanrhaeadr-yng-Nghinmeirch

they were first plucked from their native bows. The body of this lady was exhumed about three years afterwards (in 1841) and was nearly in the same state of preservation. This was confirmed by the Mayor of Ruthin."

This astonishing occurrence, which some have explained away as being due to a highly acidic soil, killing the bacteria which would otherwise cause decay, led to many pilgrims flocking to the village to pay their respects to the woman, whom they believed must have been divine.

However, it is not the spirit of Ann Parry which haunts Llanrhaeadr, but that of the wicked Dafydd Salusbury. Dafydd Salusbury was so evil that his spirit was condemned to remain on Earth till Judgement Day and, it is said, he is still to be seen — and heard — riding round and round the village at midnight on a white horse, groaning horribly. An ancient Welsh ballad entitled 'Ysbryd Dafydd Salbri' tells the story of the unhappy spirit.

In his *Highways and Byways of North Wales* (1901), A. G. Bradley tells of a haunted house near to the ancient seat of Bachymbyd, just outside the village. The house, he says, was so agressively haunted by the spirit of an old man that when it came on the market and was proposed as a suitable place for "a certain institution," the authorities wouldn't allow it, refusing to allow the prospective inmates to suffer "such terror as was said to be abroad." Bradley states that this happened a little while before writing his book.

Llandysilio

One night, many years ago, a man asleep in his home near Llandysilio Church in the Vale of Llangollen suddenly woke up to find a stranger in his room, beckoning to him. A yell of indignation froze in his throat when he realised the figure was an apparition. Its beckoning finger led him from the room and he followed the spirit down to the church, which he saw was standing open. The spectre vanished, and the curious villager crept cautiously up to the church. A ghostly light shone from the windows and voices could be heard faintly within.

The voices belonged to spirits, and they proceeded to denounce the owner of Llandysilio Hall. They said that he would not die a natural death and that a stranger would take over the hall. The awestruck man crept nervously away, and then ran as fast as he could back to his cottage. The following morning an excited group of villagers gathered under the yew trees to hear his remarkable story. For months there was scarcely any talk around Llandysilio which was not concerned with the prediction. But it was some time before the prediction came true. Many years rolled by and it became largely forgotten. Then, one day, the squire of Llandysilio Hall cut his finger on a broken wine bottle. The wound was obstinate and would not heal. He went away from home, but the hand grew worse. Shortly he died, and the first part of the prediction was thus realised . . .

On the day of the funeral a man in military attire, a stranger, turned up to attend the service. However, when the funeral procession set out, he did not join it. On returning to the hall after the service, the villagers found the door locked and barred. The stranger had taken possession! He claimed that he had won the hall as a gambling debt. And so the second part of the prophecy was fulfilled . . .

This story appeared in the *Methodist Recorder* for Christmas 1892, recounted by Rev. John S. Simon, who had heard it from his father, the Rev. John Simon, a well-known preacher in the Vale of Llangollen. Several years later, however, a sequel to the tale was added by a local person in a letter to a newspaper.

According to the story, after the squire was laid to rest and the military man was resident in the hall, the will was found to be missing. An old

Llandysilio Church, where a company of spirits were overheard prophesying the unnatural death of the local squire

woman declared that the will had been placed inside the coffin and interred with the squire. A band of villagers, anxious to remove the stranger, believed the woman's tale and so got together at midnight to dig up the body. But as the first spade dug into the fresh soil, an unearthly voice cried out over the churchyard and frightened them all off. Several were later made to appear in court, charged with attempting an illegal exhumation, and were severely reprimanded!

Llanynys

A couple of hundred years ago the parish of Llanynys near Denbigh was a treacherous place at night. Low lying, it was virtually a swamp, and dangerous bogs lay at intervals just yards from the few paths that traversed it. (The name Llanynys means "church on the island.") An excise man who one evening lost his way in a fog while crossing the marsh was therefore more than a little concerned for his safety. He could scarcely see beyond his horse's nose, and knew that if he did not find lodging soon, they may both stumble into the deadly embrace of a quagmire.

After what seemed an age, however, he finally spotted a light through the mist and gingerly directed his horse towards it. The light revealed itself to belong to a little cottage standing beside a ruined mill. He hammered on the cottage door, and it was opened by a wiry, filthy little man who in no uncertain terms told him to be off.

"I don't have lodgers here!" he said. However, the excise man finally convinced him to allow him shelter and the mean individual reluctantly allowed him the use of a small room downstairs and a ruined stable for his mount — all for an exorbitant lodging fee. Unbeknownst to the excise man, the cottage owner was loathed by his neighbours as a cruel miser believed to have a store of money hidden somewhere within his grimy home. What's more, his cottage was popularly believed to be haunted.

Yet none of this would have put off the lodger, who, cold and exhausted, was simply grateful to have found somewhere to shelter without suffering mishap in the lonesome country outside. After eating a small piece of bread and cheese, he settled down to sleep. He seemed hardly to have shut his eyes, however, when he suddenly woke up, with a strong feeling that someone else was in his room. He thought at first it might be the old man come to rob him, but on lighting a candle he found the room empty. So, a little bemused, he settled down to sleep. But again, after a short while, the same thing happened — he was disturbed by a sense of presence, although there was no-one to be seen. It happened a third time, but on this occasion the excise man could make out a figure in the corner of his room. It appeared to be wearing a Jew's gaberdine. It glided out, and the excise man felt compelled to follow.

He was startled to see the figure float through the kitchen door without opening it, and then realised that this was no ordinary intruder. He hurried outside, just in time to see the ghost glide across the stableyard. He followed, and it lingered, as if waiting for him, in one corner. As he approached, it vanished. Vowing to get to the bottom of this mystery, the excise man marked the site of the phantom's disappearance with a stick.

The next morning, the sun risen and the fog evaporated, the excise man got his bearings and rode away to Denbigh, without waking the old man. As soon as he reached the town he recounted his strange story to the beadle, and together they returned to Llanynys. They dug down where the excise man had marked the ground, and found that it covered the site of an old well. And at the bottom of the well they discovered the mouldering body of a Jewish merchant!

The old miser was swiftly made to confess his crime. He explained that the merchant, many years before, had become lost in the marsh as the excise man had done and had similarly requested lodging. He had then murdered him while he slept, stealing the expensive goods which he carried with him. The miser was shortly afterwards hanged at Denbigh for his crime, and his home, Mill House Cottage, fell into ruin.

Marford

The village of Marford near Wrexham is famous for the quaint, "gingerbread" style of its houses. The charming, doll's house designs, which delight thousands of visitors every year, were not constructed out of mere fancy, however, but for a purpose; a purpose which recalls a tragic tale — a tale of betrayal, murder and vengeance from beyond the grave! When they were built on the estate of the Trevors of Trevalyn Hall in the early years of the 19th Century, each house was adorned with a cross, fixed to the walls or in the form of cruciform windows. They were incorporated into the design to ward off a wandering ghost, the spirit of "the Lady Blackbird."

In 1713, Madam Margaret Blackbourne of Rofft Hall, now replaced by Rofft Castle, was brutally murdered by her womanising husband, George

Crucifixes and eyes are incorporated into the design of this cottage at Marford to avert evil — and the attentions of the spirit of "The Lady Blackbird"

Blackbourne, the Steward of Marford and Hosely. Some say Margaret was waylaid by him in nearby Pant Woods, others that he threw her down the stairs in a drunken rage while being tearfully questioned over some extramarital affair. Either way, the coroner, a relative of George's, brought a verdict of misadventure, and the murder went unpunished. George took a new, young wife six months later and brought her to live with him at the hall. But from that day the couple were to find no peace together . . .

Margaret Blackbourne's corpse clawed its way out of its coffin and stalked off towards Rofft Hall. As it passed through Marford, it stopped at each house in turn and tapped pathetically at a window. The startled occupants were terrified to see Margaret's pale face peering through the glass, its hair awry, its dead eyes staring. Once through the village, Margaret proceeded on to her former home, where she wandered the corridors, moaning ceaselessly until she found the wedding chamber. Here she loitered outside the door until dawn. Each night from then on Margaret repeated her folorn journey, and the villagers barricaded themselves behind closed doors. George Blackbourne and his wife moved to Trevalyn Hall at Rossett a few miles away, but the corpse of his vengeful victim followed him there, too.

Eventually, an archdeacon was called in to pray down the ghost, but he was only partly successful. Although her corpse remained at rest, her spirit, apparently, still continued to roam abroad, hence the need for the crosses built into the Marford houses. Over the years the tragic history of Madam Margaret Blackbourne passed into legend, and now her ghost is known as that of 'Lady Blackbird'.

Mold

Mold, modern Clwyd's county town, has a history which predates the Romans. The centrepiece of the town is its Bailey Hill, a partly natural, partly man-made formation which rises above the elegant Gothic parish church of St Mary to provide a landmark for miles around. It gave its name to the Celtic settlement, Yr Wyddgrug ('the green mound'), and to the English one — Mold being a corruption of Mont Altus, the name the Romans gave to the hill. Ancient skeletons are occasionally dug up in gardens bordering the Bailey Hill, and there are many rumours of ghostly figures seen flitting around its ramparts.

Below the hill stands a terrace of four Victorian houses, each apparently as haunted as the next. Siân Roadhouse lives in No.4, closest to the Bailey, and in her garden wall are remnants of Mold's original 13th century church, which was destroyed when the present church was built. A chunk of Gothic masonry, perhaps forming part of a window, is set beside four carved heads of a distinctly Celtic design, and they serve as reminders that the houses are situated in the oldest part of the town; the earliest settlement would have been round the motte and bailey. Perhaps it is the age of this land which has given the houses built upon it such supernatural sensitivity.

No.4 has been troubled by ghostly activity of a varied, and often frightening, nature for some years. They have centred most recently on a bedroom at the top of the stairs.

"It's one of the rooms we use for paying guests," said Siân, "and one or two have felt a presence in there recently. C . . . , a young girl, one of our lodgers, I remember coming downstairs one morning for breakfast looking a little pale, and I asked if she'd had a good night. 'No,' she said, 'I was woken up in the middle of the night with this eerie feeling there was someone in the room with me, and then the bed started shaking! I've been awake ever since with the light on.' I offered her another room, but she said no, she'd rather stay there — she found it all fascinating! Similar things happened for the next couple of nights and then nothing more."

The window of another room, one which would once have been used by the maid of the Victorian household, refused to stay closed. For months

Mold's haunted terrace, peaceful on a summer's day . . .

There are spirits after hours at the Boar's Head in Mold!

Siân would find it open every Saturday morning, having been opened mysteriously every Friday night. Siân tried sticking sellotape over the latch to keep it shut, but to no avail — it would be found open in the morning just the same. Siân took up the story:

"While this was going on, a lodger moved into the room and he had quite a startling experience one night. He was woken up by a knocking on the window, a kind of rapping. Then suddenly the window slammed open, and it banged about, backwards and forwards, backwards and forwards. He jumped out of bed in consternation — and then caught a glimpse of a figure disappearing downstairs, who we don't know."

Strange phenomena occur all over the house, however, and at all times of day. One afternoon, for example, Siân was having a cup of tea and a chat in the kitchen with neighbour Joyce Christopher, when Joyce suddenly exclaimed: "Look! Look at the ashtray!" Siân looked down and, with Joyce, watched the ashtray slide six inches across the table, all by itself. Items have a habit of moving about in Siân's house, but this was the first time she had actually caught one in the act! Ornaments frequently fling themselves off shelves, or are found lying on the floor, where they have fallen. Most recently, it was a large, old teddy bear which tried a taste of freedom. It leapt from its accustomed place on top of a cupboard in Siân's bedroom and landed on her while she was brushing her hair.

Of all the rooms in the house, it is this, Siân's bedroom, which seems the most haunted — and the most frighteningly so. A few years ago Siân became the victim of some malignant entity which would come to her during the darkest hours of the night. She told me: "The first time it came I woke up to find myself struggling with this thing. I couldn't physically feel anything, but there was this great pressure upon me, all down my left side. It was if something was trying to push me out, or, worse, trying to get in — get inside me. It was horrible. I struggled and struggled and felt as if all the life was being drained out of me. Desperately, I tried to remember all the prayers I knew, and just started repeating them over and over again. Finally, the pressure seemed to relax and ease off.

"I thought I'd got rid of it, I thought I'd won. But I was wrong. The thing seemed to move behind me and I felt these fingers on my shoulders. Two hands grabbed me and tried to pull me out of bed! I thought 'This is it, I'm going to die,' but then I heard this loud, awful groan from somewhere above me, and then it, whatever it was, let go. I saw this little black blob, like a black squash ball, roll away from me and vanish somewhere near the fireplace. And that was it, I was free of it. But it took me a long time to get over the shock. I had the vicar in, and he told me some prayers to say, but I'd stay up night after night, not daring to go to bed. Sometimes even now I can feel it returning, this pressure bearing down, but I've learnt to fight it off now before it starts. I don't think it'll be able to get at me again."

Siân is a brave lady indeed. The above experiences would have been quite enough to set me running from that house never to return, but Siân is clearly made of sterner stuff, as evinced by her final tale, one which made me shiver all over at the recounting of it! Siân had been lying in bed, dozing off, when she felt someone poking her in the ribs, and there came a girlish giggle from beside her. Siân rolled over to encounter someone in her bed!

"It was a young woman with a pointy face and frizzy ginger hair," said Siân, "and she was just lying there laughing at me, and prodding me, like she was teasing me. Well, I'm used to *anything* in this house by now, and I was more indignant than frightened, so I just told her to '(expletive deleted) off' and rolled over and ignored her. She disappeared."

Siân has certainly claimed more than her fair share of apparitions but her neighbours can claim a few, too. When Siân was having some renovations done on her home, her next door neighbour came round to complain — for an unusual reason.

"How long is your building work going on?" Siân was asked. "It's just that ever since they began, we've had this man in a flat cap walk through your bedroom wall, into our room, and sit on our bed! We'll be quite relieved when he stops it!"

Fellow neighbour, Joyce Christopher, checked with her sister, who had lived in the house some years previously, to discover whether she had experienced anything supernatural there. Sure enough, came the reply that indeed she had — she used to see "this little man with a cap walking about."

Joyce's house, too, has it's ghosts. Her son, Simon, once saw the phantom of an old woman in a nightie, with pince nez on her nose, and a mob cap on her head, standing in Joyce's bedroom.

"She was all grey and white, like a television," said Simon, "but she was glowing. And she was quivering all over like a jelly. I ran downstairs as soon as I saw her."

Simon had another supernatural experience in his own room. For several weeks, every night without fail, Simon would see a strange shadow on his wall:

"It was just a silhouette and two-dimensional," he said, "but it was very clear. It was a man in like a top hat, with coat tails hanging down, sitting at a very high desk. There was nothing threatening about him, he just sat there writing with a quill, but it absolutely terrified me, and I'd hide under the bedclothes. But the worst thing was that the shadow would be there when I went to sleep and would still be there when I woke up next morning. Finally, mum put me in another room. I just couldn't sleep in that one."

For a while the ghosts have been quiet. But as Joyce said: "No.1's standing empty right now, and I reckon they've all gone to live there. You wait 'till someone moves in — they'll be back!"

Between the Bailey Hill and the church is a rather unlikely setting for a haunting — a chip shop. It is haunted by the spirit of an old man. Mr Arthur Polly, the owner of the chip shop in 1973, told the *Flintshire Leader* newspaper that the apparition always left behind "a strange sensation" after being seen, and he believed it to be a death omen. After the first sighting of the ghost, an aunt died and after its final appearance a relative was killed in a road accident. Mr Polly added that the chippy's previous owner frequently heard "bumps in the night," although he saw no ghost, and a next-door-neighbour would often hear inexplicable noises coming from the building during the night.

In contrast to its modern usage, the building which houses the chippy is a very old one, and was once used as a court house. It is possible that the spirit which haunts it is the shade of a former felon, condemned for some long-forgotten crime.

In the centre of the town, Thompson's Stores, a tobacconists with an attractive black and white frontage, is all that remains of Cambrian House, a 17th century family home and one-time doctor's surgery. Thompson's Stores was once the servants' quarters and surgery itself. A servant girl who died in the house has long been said to haunt the shop, although she has not been seen for some years. Tradition has it that the girl died of smallpox and that her pitiful, pock-marked face would peer out of the window overlooking Earl Road. This window has since been whitewashed over.

Owner Richard Perry has heard a slightly different account: "There's no evidence to suggest she suffered from smallpox," he told me, "but it certainly seems she was very ill and confined by the doctor to the room upstairs. I believe she fell from the window, meeting her death on the cobbles below, though whether this was deliberate or not, no-one knows."

Another black and white building, the *Boar's Head* pub, near the bus station, also has its resident ghost, an indistinct, misty figure which materialises near the former lounge door, now bricked up as part of a renovation programme, and drifts through the bar after closing time. Licensee Mr Philip Armishaw has never seen it but his teenage sons, Matthew and Daniel, have. Mr Armishaw told me:

"It always seems to appear after closing time, while we're tidying up or relaxing over a coffee. The bar staff have often seen it and once my son, Matthew, said to me: 'Dad, someone's just come into the lounge,' which seemed odd, because everything was locked up, and, sure enough, when I went to look there was nobody there."

One witness described the phantom as "the fog-like shape of a man." The room often goes cold before it makes an appearance. Daniel informed me that it was a more frequent visitor before the renovations were carried out, and he saw it himself passing by the hatchway which once opened into the old lounge bar. The figure always disappears in the direction of the old living quarters, which makes Mr Armishaw think it might be the ghost of a former landlord.

His wife, Gaynor, had an unsettling experience recently (1991), when, as she was just about to get into her bath, a mirror on the wall suddenly leapt across the room, smashing against the floor. Perhaps the phantom had been helping itself to a few pints for old time's sake and got a little over-boisterous!

A former vicar of Mold, the Rev. J. J. Morgan, had an unnerving adventure on the hill now crowned by Theatr Clwyd. This land was part of the Llwynegrin estate, and the old hall is now all but hidden by the modern complex of Shire Hall, the County Library Headquarters and the Crown Courts. In the Rev. Morgan's day, however, the hill was a lonely spot, with an eerie reputation. He recounted his adventure in his 1949 autobiography, *A welais ac a glywais:*

He had been preaching in a chapel in Northop (Llaneurgain), and was detained until rather late. Returning home, and passing Llwynegrin Hall, he noticed a man and a woman sitting on a stile in the hedge by a house called Glasfryn. They were huddled closely together, obviously young lovers, and the vicar saw the man putting his arm around the girl's shoulders. But then he realised that this was no lover's embrace — for, flashing in the moonlight, he saw the blade of a dagger! The man plunged the knife through the girl's hair and deep into her throat. She let out an unearthly scream, and the Rev. Morgan, believing himself the witness to a murder, rushed over . . . but he found the stile empty, and the couple nowhere to be seen.

Another hill on the outskirts of Mold, Bryn yr Ellyllon (or 'Hill of the Goblins'), has also justified its haunted reputation. For centuries tales had been told of a giant phantom, called the Brenin yr Allt ("King of the Hillside"), which roamed the area around a burial mound on the hill. A woman who encountered the spectre in the 18th century was driven mad at the sight of it.

"It was," she said, "glittering and shining in gold."

In 1830, a farmwife returning home from Mold market was making her way up Bryn yr Ellyllon when she saw a weird golden glow emanating from the woods on one side of her. Suddenly, out of the trees strode a huge man clad in ancient armour, apparently made entirely of gold. His whole body seemed surrounded by light as he crossed her path. He vanished into the burial mound and the light was extinguished. The woman was so alarmed that she immediately returned to Mold to tell the vicar all about it. He took down her account and had several people witness it.

Three years later, some solid evidence to prove the truth of her story was found when the mound was broken into during road widening. Inside was found a prehistoric grave, and the tall skeleton of a man. About its shoulders was a large cape of purest gold! This cape, the largest piece of worked Bronze Age gold to be found in Europe, is now on prominent display in the British Museum. Unfortunately, it suffered rather at the hands of the finders, who tore chunks away to melt down for jewellery. But, it is said, ill fortune followed all those who had disturbed the grave, and many felt the presence of the Brenin yr Allt dogging their footsteps.

The Ancient King may yet still haunt the area, or so the disturbing experience of student Paul Adams, of Sychdyn, suggests. Mr Adams was walking home across the rugby field which adjoins the site of the burial mound (now obscured by house building) one night in December, 1988, when he heard the sound of footsteps approaching him. He peered through the darkness but was unable to see anyone.

"I stopped to wait for whoever it was to appear," Mr Adams explained, "but then the footsteps stopped, too. I listened for a bit, and then continued — and the footsteps immediately started up again, just a few yards ahead of me. They had a strange sound to them, a crunching, as if whoever was making them was walking on frosty ground. But there was no frost underfoot at all.

"There was something very eerie about this, so I decided to head back the way I'd come. But as I turned round, the footsteps seemed to follow. Suddenly, they were ahead of me again, approaching from the opposite direction! Immediately, I turned back, but still they came on. I turned again — and there they were still coming toward me. I was really scared by this time and the footsteps started walking round and round me, continually, hemming me in. Finally, I just ran for it, I've no intention of walking home that way again!"

Near the stately home of Rhual, on the way to Gwernaffield, there once stood a well enclosed in a grove of trees. It was called the Goblin Well and was believed to be haunted by a bwbach, or evil spirit. In the 1840's a young man encountered this bwbach while returning home after a night visiting his girlfriend, a barmaid at a Mold pub. He had walked the road many times, and although he had felt a shiver of anticipation each time he passed the well, nothing had ever materialised to frighten him, and so he soon made up his mind that it wasn't haunted after all.

One night, however, he met a strange woman on the road, enrobed in a glowing white gown, the hood pulled up, hiding her face. She asked him to accompany her.

"I am frightened to walk the road alone," she said. "The well is supposed to be haunted, isn't it?"

The young man agreed that it was, although he had never seen anything, and gallantly he agreed to join her side. He glanced inside the hood, to examine the face of his new companion — but could see only blackness. He stared harder, but still could see no face . . . and then the horrible truth dawned on him!

"You've got no head!" he yelped. The faceless hood laughed a silvery laugh, and replied: "No indeed, but fear not, if you fetch a pick and shovel I can show you where a fabulous treasure is buried under the well, and it can all be yours! All, that is, except my necklace. It's important I have my necklace," she continued, "because it will help to fasten my head back onto my shoulders, just like it was before they hacked it off in a sacrifice and buried me with the treasure."

But she had lost her audience. The young man was already running as fast as he could up the hill, and screaming all the way! The bwbach, furious at such rudeness, transformed herself into a ball of fire and chased after him, bumping up against his breeches and scorching his behind, all the way to his front door.

That's the legend, but tradition says there may be a much more down-to-earth explanation for the tale. The father of the young man's girlfriend, it is said, did not approve of the relationship, and in order to frighten the youth from travelling every night to visit her, as he had been wont to do, he masqueraded as the spirit of the Goblin Well — with a white sheet and a turnip under his arm as a severed head! The drunken youth later embellished the story in its telling.

The ghost may not be all imagination, however. A white lady is still said to haunt the road where the Goblin Well was once situated. I have been told that she was recently encountered by some men fixing a tyre of a car which had broken down there.

Mynydd Hiraethog

Hiraeth is a word with no equivalent in English. It embodies a sense of longing, loneliness, homesickness, of spiritual Welshness. It is a haunting word. Clwyd's expanse of stark but beautiful moorland, called prosaically in English the Denbigh Moors, bears in Welsh the name Mynydd Hiraethog; and is an area of especial atmosphere. It is rich in folklore and strange tales of the supernatural. Here spectral black dogs have been encountered, unearthly singing heard ringing from the sky, fairies and UFOs seen, and numerous mysterious ancient monuments pock-mark the landscape, each with its own tradition.

The most familiar landmark on the moors is the ruined shell of Gwylfa Hiraethog, a hunting lodge destroyed by fire earlier this century. Schoolchildren refer to it as "the haunted house" or "Dracula's castle" because of its eerie aspect, but in fact there is no substantiated ghost story attached to it. However, a few hundred yards away, a more modest structure, a little stone bridge, is the haunt of one of the county's most venerable phantoms — that of a Roman soldier. Why he haunts the bridge is unknown. Perhaps he was set to guard it and was slain by Welsh resistence fighters during the Roman invasion.

However, one thing is certain, says Jane Pugh in her *Welsh Ghosts, Poltergeists and Demons*, his appearance is an omen of death. The author describes two recent encounters with the centurion, who materialised, mist-like, his plumed helmet clearly visible, a sword raised above his head. In each case, one member of the party who saw him died soon after, one of an alleged heart attack, another in a rock fall at a quarry.

Mynydd Isa

The first indication Geoff Ellis had that his new home was haunted was when he heard his dog trotting upstairs.

"Misty!" he yelled. "Get back down here at once!"

"I don't know what you're shouting for," replied his wife, Viv, "Misty's sitting at your feet."

And so he was . . . looking up at Geoff's surprised face with a hurt expression. Since then, the ghost dog of Primrose Cottage, and its phantom companions, have become so much a part of Geoff's family that he has become almost blasé about them.

When Geoff bought Primrose Cottage it was a shell, three old cottages knocked into one, and requiring a great deal of renovation. But Geoff fell in love with it immediately.

"It had such a good atmosphere, so welcoming," Geoff told me, "that I knew we'd be happy here, and we have been."

He continued: "There's nothing threatening about the ghosts. In fact, I'm sure my little girl plays with the dog. She'll chuckle away for hours in an empty room, having fun with someone. I don't often see it myself, usually just hear it pattering upstairs, but occasionally I get a glimpse of it walking through the living room. It's an indistinct shape and usually has someone with it, either a little old woman or a man. It's difficult to be certain, because the image is so shadowy, like a glimpse out of the corner of your eye — look again and they'll be gone."

A tall male figure wearing a grey sweater is also sometimes seen passing by a door into the kitchen from the hall. This may be the man seen accompanying the dog, or another apparition altogether. Either way, he bears similarities with the others in that he is a shadowy, featureless figure, harmless, silent and anonymous. Presumably, all three or four ghosts are those of former occupants of the cottages, but from which period is unknown. Geoff does not seem too curious about his mysterious tenants; he is happy to leave them in peace, if they do him. Unfortunately, this is not always the case — the ghosts enjoy playing the occasional prank on Geoff and his family!

"Things disappear," Geoff explained, grimly. "You put things down, go to get them, and they've gone. It happened recently with my wife's purse. Viv put it down by the telephone, and a minute later it had gone. Of course, she was frantic, it contained all her money, car keys, the lot. She roped everyone in to search, and the house was turned upside down! And then, after a day of searching, suddenly there it was, back, just where she'd left it, by the phone. It's infuriating!

"Actually," he added, "I had a very peculiar experience once when I was using the phone. I was alone in the house, in the middle of a conversation, when I suddenly felt a hand pinch my bum! Made me jump, I can tell you! You wouldn't think a ghost would do that, would you? But I suppose they have to get their fun somehow."

However extraordinary that experience may have been, this is not the end of Primrose Cottage's mysteries. Most enigmatic of all is the inexplicable whistling which can sometimes be heard from the bathroom. Geoff is convinced it has an intelligence behind it, for it seems to warn of impending accidents. The family have learned to take notice of it.

Gary Tolley, Geoff's brother-in-law, was one of the first to hear it. He said: "While we were doing up the house I was drilling through a wall in the kitchen when I suddenly heard this strange whistling coming from the bathroom upstairs. The house was a shell so I could hear it echoing downstairs quite easily. A moment later I drilled through a wire, and got an electric shock! On another occasion, David, Geoff's eldest son, was wiring into a wall, when we heard the whistling again. Seconds later he shorted the house out with his screwdriver.

"I'm sure the sound is meant as a warning. We don't hear it so often now, but we did quite a few times while we were doing the building work. Once, we had been working through the night, and I'd gone outside for a smoke, when Geoff and the others heard the whistling again. By this time, they'd learnt to take notice of it, so they scurried around trying to find out what was up. They came looking for me and there I was, so tired I'd fallen asleep standing up — my cigarette burning down to my fingers."

There seems no explanation for the warning whistle, but one thing all are agreed on — it doesn't sound human.

"It's more like a bird call," said Gary, "a warbling noise, like someone trying to do an impression of a bird. It's very peculiar, unearthly. But it's proved useful!"

The common conception of what a haunted house should be is done away with completely when one enters Primrose Cottage. A bright and happy home, it is anything but eerie. One can hardly blame a few departed souls for wishing to linger on here, in such a warm and welcoming atmosphere.

Nannerch

Moel Arthur, a windswept, heather-clad hill in the Clwydian Range, is believed to be named after King Arthur, who, local legend states, ruled Britain from the ancient hillfort on its summit. Possibly, he was buried here also, for a burial chamber called Cist Arthur, or Arthur's Vault, was discovered on the hill in the 18th century. Unfortunately, its location has since been lost — unfortunate because it may contain fabulous riches! A great treasure is said to have been interred somewhere on Moel Arthur, and where better than in the tomb of Britain's first Christian king?

Although it has occasionally been located, this treasure has proved impossible to claim. A supernatural white light conveniently marks its secret site each midnight, but anyone attempting to dig at the spot has been driven away by sudden, violent storms, or, worse still, has been approached by the Grey Lady, the cache's spectral guardian, a statuesque, white-faced apparition, whose eyes have the power to kill at a glance. The Grey Lady treats would-be prospectors mercilessly, frightening them to death with one glare from her awful eyes. But she has been known to be compassionate towards the innocent. One night a poor man encountered her after becoming lost on the mountain, and, while he carefully kept his gaze fixed firmly to the ground, and humbly apologised for trespass, she pressed three dry peas into his hand — which, when he eventually found his way home, he discovered had been transformed into solid gold!

King Arthur's treasure remains undiscovered, and so we must assume the Grey Lady still roams the mountainside, on the look-out for those aiming to disturb the grave — and risk the consequences!

While the Grey Lady patrols the hills above Nannerch, in the valley below it is a Black Lady who frightens the living. Her haunt is a stretch of road between Nannerch and the village of Afonwen. There is little known about her. In fact, until I met the most recent witness of her appearance, tourism information officer Alan Williams, I did not know of her existence. Nothing had been written about her, and neither myself nor Alan knew of other witnesses. This is what Alan told me of his encounter:

"My mate and I were on our way to the pub in Nannerch — and I stress *to*, neither of us had had a drop — when suddenly this woman just came

Wild Moel Arthur, bearing the ramparts of its Iron Age hillfort, is patrolled by a dangerous Grey Lady

out in front of me, as if from the hedge. I stepped back, startled, and muttered an apology and said to my mate: 'Why didn't you warn me about that woman?' 'What woman?' he replied. He hadn't seen her, just me. And, of course, she'd vanished.''

In the split second that the figure took to pass in front of him, Alan caught a glimpse of a head bowed, hidden by a hood, apparently staring into a book. The attire was that which may have been worn by any Victorian lady. Some time after his experience, Alan heard from a relative that there was an old story of a woman who had been killed — in some unspecified manner — on her way to church, and who now haunted the road. That was all he knew which might substantiate his tale. I printed his story in my *History and Mystery* column, running through several papers, and we waited to see if any other witnesses would come forward. We didn't have to wait long — the response was almost immediate.

Mrs Vera Jones of Rhuddlan wrote to tell of her late husband's encounter with the ghost. She said: "My late husband was the village constable at Nannerch from 1951 to 1961. One winter's night, when on duty, he was walking towards the Wheeler Hill when suddenly this lady walked towards him, then suddenly vanished into the hedge. He shone his powerful torch, called out something, but there was not a sight or sound of anyone. Her attire was as you mention, rather Victorian, wearing head gear."

Mr H. Donnel of Buckley repeated an account by his father of an encounter with the ghost, which took place shortly after the First World War: "One evening he was approaching the Rising Sun Inn [on his bike] when a lady dressed in long, Victorian clothes, but whose face was hidden, suddenly stepped out in front of him. He swerved so violently that he fell off his machine, but when he turned round, the lady had completely vanished.

"Despite ridicule from others, I took my Dad's story seriously, and recall that in the early 1930's he and I paid a visit on our bikes and he showed me the exact spot where he had seen the lady. I vividly remember that in those days there was, in the hedge, the rotted remains of an old garden gate and some yards back the just discernible ruins of an old cottage, overgrown with trees and bushes. It was from the gate that the lady stepped in front of my father."

I printed these letters in *History and Mystery*, and a fortnight later received another, from a 75-year-old woman in Buckley. Her father, as a young man, in 1904, took a pony and trap along the haunted road to attend a party. His father warned him to return early, in case they encountered the ghost — and he didn't want the horse frightened! However, youth being what it is, he forgot, and what should happen but . . .

"The horse suddenly made an awful noise and bolted. My dad said coming toward them was a white mist and as they went forward a great chill came over them and then it vanished. Looking round they saw this woman in a flowing cloak go into the hedge. The horse never stopped galloping until it got home to the stable, and it was covered with sweat and lather and was frightened to death."

This story suggests that the ghost was already established by the early years of this century. If her attire is truly late Victorian, then she must have begun to haunt the road shortly after her death. The ruined cottage Mr Donnel mentions may be assumed to be where she lived. There is no trace of it today. Alan Williams was delighted to receive some confirmation of his story to show doubting friends — and I was more than delighted to have been involved in uncovering and substantiating a haunting which may otherwise have escaped recording.

Pentrefoelas

The squire of Pentrefoelas was a hard man who ruled the village with a rod of iron. He would have no truck with charity, beggars or old people, and held onto his own wealth jealously. Any form of trespass against him was severely punished. It was therefore with a great deal of relief, not to say joy in some quarters, that the news was received of the squire's death (one year in the 18th century). Foelas estate was thrown into confusion while the installation of the new squire was underway, and some young bloods of the village decided it was about time they got their own back on the miserly old squire by stealing some of his produce. They decided to go scrumping.

Prior to the squire's death, his orchard was constantly guarded by gamekeepers, but on the particular moonlit night the youths chose for their escapade, it was deserted, the keepers too occupied with the wine from his cellars and the maids from his kitchen to care about their former duties. Choosing a tree heavily laden with tempting fruit, the young men clambered into its branches and started knocking the apples onto the ground, for later collection. Suddenly, one of their number gave a cry of alarm.

"It's the squire!" he squeaked. Below them could be clearly seen the familiar tricorn hat of the squire of Foelas. But alarm turned to frank terror when they all as one remembered an important fact — the squire was dead! Yelling wildly, the boys dropped from the tree and ran for their lives. Soon they reached the road, and, panting for breath, began to congratulate themselves on a lucky escape. But who should they then see, standing in the road, leaning on his staff and frowning murderously at them, but the ghostly squire! Charging away as fast as their legs could carry them, the would-be scrumpers eventually made it to their homes unmolested. And the dead squire's orchards remained unmolested, too — for as long as the tale of his unexpected return was repeated around the village.

Not far from Pentrefoelas, near the ancient house of Cernioge Mawr, there was a haunted ruin. A spectral black pig would often be seen coming

Pentrefoelas — where rash youths were terrified by the restless spirit of their dead squire

from the ruin and wandering away down the lane that passed it, often in broad daylight. The local people became quite used to it, for it would frequently follow them down the road. Attempts to dissuade it would be in vain. Occasionally, a disgruntled person would lash out at it with their stick, but the stick would pass straight through it, and the phantom sow would continue on its journey regardless, finally vanishing as mysteriously as it had appeared.

Pontblyddyn

So much has been written before on Plas Teg that there is little this book can add. Clwyd's most famous (or infamous) haunted house, Plas Teg ('the Fair Mansion') stands beside the dual carriageway linking Mold and Wrexham, a little outside the village of Pontblyddyn. Built in 1610 by John Trevor, it is a rare example of a Jacobean mansion, four-square solid but elegant, with fine turrets at each corner. Recently restored at great expense by interior designer Cornelia Bayley, Plas Teg was virtually a ruin a few years ago, but now it, and its several mysterious features, including a secret compartment in the staircase, witch marks in the chimney breast, and two haunted bedrooms, can be admired again.

Many are the apparitions and inexplicable happenings experienced at Plas Teg. Its best known ghosts are those of a young girl who drowned in the well in the 17th century, and that of her distraught lover, who hanged himself in his grief. The unfortunate girl has been most often seen, a pathetic figure in a long, white dress, but her lover most often heard. His heavy, masculine tread frequently echoes along the landing, and he has been known to hammer furiously at bedroom doors.

The chamber generally pointed out as the "haunted room" is the Regency Room on the first floor, but the Twin Posters room on the second is also haunted, and, for me, possesses a much more sinister atmosphere, tense and claustrophobic. Even scarier is a ground floor room, the base of one of the turrets, which was once used to hang felons when Plas Teg was used as the local court house. Accountant Mark Ridgeway, who slept for a time in this room, told me that he would often wake up to feel a presence in the room. Sometimes he would wake with the unhappy impression that *something* was staring at him — a few inches from his face — invisible in the darkness. Once he distinctly felt something sit beside him on the bed, which sank down on one side. He shortly found alternative lodging!

Strange lights and unearthly screams have also been reported in the vicinity of Plas Teg, but strangest of all are the phantom horsemen which are said to haunt the highway every autumn. Three in number, they patrol the wooded section of the dual carriageway at dusk. In previous centuries they have pursued travellers on the road and harrassed poachers in the woods, but there is no tale to account for their presence and their identity remains a mystery.

Prestatyn

Despite its brash, modern image as a popular seaside town, with caravan parks and gift shops, Prestatyn possesses considerable history. Possibly the earliest inhabited place in North Wales, Prestatyn was later the site of a thriving Roman community, and archaeological digs have revealed remains of their occupation. The town also has more than its share of hauntings. Journalist and historian Harry Thomas, who lives in the town, has investigated many of them, and it is he I must thank for my information on Nant Hall Road:

Nant Hall Road, which is said to have been built over a Roman cemetery, seems especially haunted. A recent visitation took place in a council flat on the top floor of number 28. A young couple applied to be rehoused after they were awoken each night by the sound of doors banging and footsteps running up and down the corridor outside their room. Friends who stayed with them also heard the noises, and a grey, misty figure was seen hovering outside their bedroom. The troubles seemed to start soon after the couple's baby was born, and a medium who was called in claimed to contact the spirit of an old woman in the flat, a former nanny who worked in the house in the early 1900's. She had been attracted to the child, the medium told the worried occupants, and the bangings were the sound of her checking the doors were locked, something she used regularly to do when alive.

The old police station in Nant Hall Road was also haunted by an old woman. A former occupant wrote to Harry Thomas to tell him of her experiences there during the 1960's, and she kindly agreed for him to pass on the letter to me. She wrote:

"I began to notice an additional member of the household who seemed to stand just to the side or behind me. I never really saw her face. I say 'her' as I feel she was an old woman, dressed in long dark clothes. I was never frightened — more a feeling of friendly company, and I was on my own a lot at night. The back kitchen and landing were her favourite haunts. None of my family were aware of her and we moved away 16 months later.

"The house became the publicity offices and I found an excuse to go in one afternoon. I mentioned I had lived there and the man looked horrified and said: 'Nothing would induce me to stay here after dark. This place is haunted!' He and I had felt the same thing in the same places."

On the sea front itself, a ghostly white nun walks, usually on summer evenings. One man had a very close encounter with her indeed, according to Jane Pugh's *Welsh Ghosts, Poltergeists and Demons*. He had been taking his dog for a walk along the pavement by the sea wall, between the Nova centre and Ffrith Beach, when he saw a figure dressed in a long white gown approach him. He did not realise at first that she was a ghost, and was therefore surprised and annoyed when his dog, rather more alert, yelped loudly and ran off in terror in the opposite direction. When he looked back, the phantom nun was almost upon him, and a sensation of extreme cold came over him. He then noticed that under the nun's wimple there was no face. Although he would then have very much liked to have followed his dog's example, and turn tail and run, he found that he could not move — his feet were rooted to the spot!

The ghost continued in her relentless stride and walked right through the unfortunate man. He felt nothing but an icy chill, and then the warmth of the evening returned to him and he found he could move again. The nun had disappeared. Cautiously, his dog sheepishly made its return, and they continued their walk — I suspect to the nearest pub!

Rhes-y-Cae

On the edge of Halkyn Mountain stands Ffagnallt Hall, an ancient farmhouse with medieval foundations and a fine Jacobean staircase. The farmer and his family share their home with an occupant perhaps even older than the house itself — the yellowed remains of a skull, reverently locked away in a glass-fronted case on the mantlepiece. A well-known legend states that this macabre relic belonged to a Welsh hero — some say Dafydd, Prince of Wales, a relation of King Henry I — who was murdered by his brother-in-law while taking refuge in the hall.

There had been a price on the hero's head and the treacherous lord of Ffagnallt had poisoned his cup, in order to claim the reward from his English overlords. But before he died, the hero cursed the house. He said that after his death, his head should be removed from his body and put in a place of honour in the house, so that the cowardly deed should never be forgotten. After the murderer had given over the corpse to the English, and he had received the bounty, his fate was sealed. His wife, his son, and, eventually, the whole court left him, and he died in madness, alone in the empty hall. His son then retrieved the hero's head, now a fleshless skull, from its spike on the gateway into Chester, and he, his mother and their retinue returned to Ffagnallt. The skull was placed in a casket on a table in the main hall where all could see it.

For many years the hall prospered, but then came a period of repeated tragedy. The heir of the hall died in a hunting accident, his sister drowned in a swamp, the crops failed and the farm animals were all found dead one morning. It was then that the casket containing the skull was found to be missing. A magician was called in to try and end the run of bad luck. He interviewed the servants, and suddenly one of them cried out in terror. An apparition of the skull was hovering above his head! The magician told the terrified man that if he told the truth the skull would not harm him. The servant explained that he had stolen the casket, guessing that it was filled with jewels. He had carried it to an outhouse, and there discovered the skull. Horrified, he took it to the churchyard and buried it. At once, the skull was retrieved and returned to its former position, thus ending the misfortune that had fallen on the house.

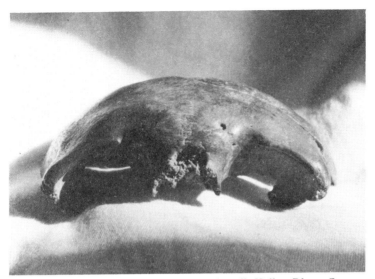

All that remains of the cursed skull of Ffagnallt Hall at Rhes-y-Cae

The skull was also removed from Ffagnallt in the 19th century by a peevish maid, anxious to be rid of the 'dusty old thing'. She threw it in the duckpond! That night bloodcurdling moans and shrieks echoed through the house, doors crashed open and closed and heavy, ghostly footsteps tramped the corridors. The maid was found in her nightie splashing about in the pond in a delirious state, searching for the skull which she had foolishly thrown out. As soon as it was found and returned to its rightful place, the creepy disturbances ceased. And, the current owners tell me, that is the way it is going to stay — they intend to make sure the skull remains peacefully in its box on the mantlepiece for as long as they live there!

Rhewl

The hamlet of Rhewl, situated above a great loop in the River Dee between Glyndyfrdwy and Llangollen, has more than its share of ghost stories. The spirit of a murdered traveller once haunted a stream near Tyntwll Farm, and was known as 'the Ghost of Rhewl'. He had been set upon by a gang of thieves desirous of the gold sovereigns he carried. In a desperate bid to save himself, he threw the coins into the stream, hoping this would divert their attention. But the robbers showed no mercy, and his sad spectre could be seen hovering about the scene of his death for many years afterwards. It was only after the sovereigns were found in the stream by the farmer that the spirit seemed to find rest and appeared no more.

Rhewl must have been rather a rough place in centuries past, for it was fear of robbers which indirectly led to another ghost becoming resident in Rhewl. A young lady travelling through the district hid her jewels and sovereigns inside a sock secreted behind the beam of the room in which she was lodging. But she died — whether by foul means or other, the story does not say — before she had the chance to retrieve them. And there they remained. And so did she, in spirit form. Just like the murdered farmer, her shade loitered around the site of her hidden treasure, until it was finally discovered, years on, after the fabric of the sock had rotted away and the jewels had spilled out onto the floor and into the light of day. It is a traditional belief that anything hidden by a person will act as a magnet to his spirit if he dies before he has reclaimed it.

War, too, with its many sudden and violent deaths, is also likely to produce ghosts. So it proved in Rhewl, where the army of Prince Llywelyn was wiped out by the forces of Henry III in 1244. The ghosts of the slain soon began to plague the villagers. They took the forms of little elves, and came out every night from Coedygadfa ('Wood of the Battle'). An old woman who lived on the edge of the wood took it upon herself to keep the phantoms at bay. At dusk she would venture into Coedygadfa, armed with a stout stick and a frying pan of cooked rabbits' and frogs' legs, the smell of which strongly resembled that of burning bodies on the battlefield. This horrible reminder of their mortal end sent the elf-like spectres cowering back under the ground!

Rhos-on-Sea

In the bright and breezy little seaside town of Rhos-on-Sea stands Cegin y Mynach (The Monk's Kitchen), which was once a grange, or outbuilding, of a 13th century Cistercian monastery, where monks would stay overnight to catch fish to feed their brethren. Formerly a family home, then a café, Cegin y Mynach is now deserted, and falling into ruin. It stands folorn in a cracked concrete courtyard and its stately presence is marred by a neglected, overgrown crazy golf course next door. As I write (1991) there is talk of demolishing it. This would indeed be a sad loss to the county, for, despite its sorry situation, the building possesses great charm as well as history, and should be saved.

The entrance to Cegin y Mynach's courtyard is flanked by two stone monks. One of these may be the likeness of a past resident of the grange who occasionally still makes his presence known. The April 1979 edition of *Country Quest* magazine tells the story of a Mr Long and his mother, who had been taking tea one afternoon in Cegin y Mynach, then still a café, when they saw a figure in a brown habit walk up the drive, enter the café and throw on a white cloak. He was stocky, of medium height, with a tonsure and a bearded face with bright eyes. He turned and vanished up the stairs. They asked the owner about him, but her only reply was "Oh, have you seen him?" and then they learnt of the sightings reported down the years of Cegin y Mynach's phantom monk.

This devout brother stands guard at the entrance of Cegin-y-Mynach, Rhos-on-Sea — is it his spirit which still haunts the place?

Rhuddlan

One of Clwyd's most impressive ancient monuments is Rhuddlan Castle, which was built by Edward I as one of a chain of fortresses intended to help suppress the Welsh. Although little more now than a shell, the castle's massive walls and towers nevertheless remain awe-inspiring memorials to the might of our feudal past. According to *Welsh Legends* published by J. Bacock in 1802, Rhuddlan Castle used to echo at night with fearful groans, screams and eerie laughter. Two spirits would be seen chasing through the ruined corridors and gaping doorways — the Princess Erilda and her hellish tormentor, the Warrior Knight of the Blood Red Plume.

Erilda, daughter of the Prince of North Wales, was to have married the Prince of South Wales, thus uniting the Principality in peace, but the plans were upset by a demon, disguising itself as a noble knight, in order that war and hatred would continue to reign. Only after he had stolen Erilda's love and persuaded her to elope did the Warrior Knight reveal his true self — a hideous, scaly monster covered in slime and creeping things! The demon stabbed the princess' heart through with a trident and cast her limp body into the River Clwyd. Then he, too, disappeared below the river's boiling surface, returning to the depths of hell from which he had come. From that night on, says the story, Erilda's spirit was doomed to be persecuted by the demon till Judgement Day, for betraying her country and her father.

In rather more recent years another ghost was seen near the castle. Mrs Margaret Hibbert, writing into my *History and Mystery* column in the *Rhyl Journal*, told me:

"My mother . . . was entertaining some friends when this ghost walked past the window. He was wearing a cloak and a wide brimmed hat and he was covered in mist. She rushed out but he had gone. She was too shocked to even speak, so she said nothing to anybody. In any case, as she said, they would only have laughed at her. But my mother was the last person to have such a vivid imagination so I have always believed it to be true."

The impressive ruins of Rhuddlan Castle, where the screaming spirit of the luckless Princess Erilda is chased by the shade of her demon lover

A host of terrifying apparitions was encountered on an old lane between the castle and Twt Hill, the site of the Norman motte and bailey. In the 1950's a miner was one evening returning to his home along the lane when suddenly he saw blocking his path a group of dwarvish men carrying picks and lamps, jabbering to each other in a strange language. They were led by three cowled figures, seven foot tall, and as they came upon him he realised he could see no faces under their hoods — just fiendish grins staring out of blackness! He lashed out at them, but they barged him sideways, forcing him through the hedge beside the lane. Scratched and bleeding, he fainted dead away.

Mrs Marie Evans of Rhuddlan informed me that in 1970 excavations carried out by Exeter University in the playing fields beside the lane revealed the site of a Norman church and a graveyard, almost directly opposite where the witness encountered the apparitions. The skeleton of a dwarf was found in one of the graves, so, who knows, perhaps more graves are yet to be discovered . . .

Rhyl

The bright bustle of a funfair would seem an unlikely place for a haunting, but on the land where the Ocean Beach fair at Rhyl now stands there was once a haunted house, Foryd Hall. Foryd was built in the early 1800s by an MP. By the 1930's it had become empty and fallen into disrepair and during the Second World War it was demolished because it had become unsafe. The hall earned its haunted reputation during the latter stages of its life, on account of a ghostly figure, dressed all in grey, which could be seen staring folornly from its lonely windows.

Prestatyn historian Harry Thomas researched the tales and discovered the ghost was believed to be that of a French nun, who met with an untimely end while living in the hall. Her history is unknown, but old people recall that a French sailor fitted somewhere into her story: probably they were lovers, despite her vows, and some tragedy overtook them. The sad nun was frequently seen by passers-by and local fishermen standing at one of the big bay windows on the second floor, waving out to sea, possibly as a warning.

Now, perhaps, when the lights of the carousels fade and the merrymakers have all gone home, the melancholy apparition of a young woman in grey materialises unobserved and still keeps her lonesome vigil, watching for a lover who can never return to her.

Rossett

If a child in Rossett stayed outdoors too long after his bedtime, it was once common to hear his mother scold: "Come inside at once — or Old Jeffrey will get you!"

Old Jeffrey was a criminal gibbetted on Rossett Green in the 17th century. He had attacked a labourer near Gresford and then run away, leaving him for dead. But the man recovered and gave testimony. Jeffrey was captured and hanged at Ruthin. His body was stapled to the gibbet at Rossett and left to rot.

The corpse was left hanging for years and the ghastly scene greatly annoyed the villagers. Its grim presence seemed to put a stigma upon the community and farmers would find that no-one would buy their produce at market. Eventually, a group of men decided to take matters into their own hands. One night they assembled at the gibbet, and, prizing apart the

The remains of a gibbett went into the fabric of an outhouse at the Golden Lion in Rossett

iron staples, took the gruesome body down, and buried it on the Green. Then, in a final act of defiance to the authorities who had ignored their problem, they broke up the gibbet.

Some of the wood from the gibbet came to be incorporated into the structure of an outbuilding of the village's *Golden Lion* pub (one of the iron staples can be clearly seen jutting out of one of the interior walls) and this may explain the ghostly activity which has been occurring at the pub over the years. So far, however, the spirit has shown none of the murderous tendencies of the unfortunate Jeffrey. Sometimes he is heard tinkling glasses behind the bar first thing in the morning, and he has been known to break one or two while no-one is looking. He has also taken a dislike to the occasional ornament or wall decoration, throwing them down from their accustomed positions. Usually, however, his is a peaceful presence, most often seen quietly standing, in ploughman's dress, in Room 2 above the lounge bar, or occasionally on the landing outside.

Ruabon

A miner hurrying home past Ruabon Church one late twilight was surprised to see a funeral procession approaching. Thinking it an unusual time of day for a funeral, he paused, curious to know whose it might be. He recognised a doctor and a few tradesmen among the mourners, and could faintly discern the sound of singing, but was unable to make out the tune. His curiosity was aroused further when the procession passed the church, and graveyard, and continued instead to a nearby house.

He thought no more of it until, a few days later, he came across the real procession, in broad daylight, exactly as he had seen it before, with the same faces in the crowd, and the same music. He realised then that he had previously been witness to an apparition, a phantom funeral. Just as he had seen it do those few nights before, the cortege passed the church and stopped outside a house, where he learnt that the body was that of a man from the south of England, and was so conveyed to his home, before being transported for burial the next day.

The imposing old school of Lindisfarne College, built on the site of Wynnstay Park, showplace of the wealthy Sir Watkin Williams Wynn, boards more than just scholars — if the local schoolchildren are to be believed. Kath Wilkinson's fourth year English class (see Acrefair, Cefn Mawr) are convinced that ghosts are also resident. The hauntings centre themselves, it seems, on the 101 foot high Wynnstay Column in the grounds. The children's stories vary considerably, and form an interesting example of how folk tales can become warped in the telling; although I imagine there is some genuine account somewhere behind the variations. Here are just a few of the children's tales:

"This is a story of Lady Harriet, who was a very wealthy lady who lived in Wynnstay Park. In those days they used to do a lot of fox hunting and horse racing. Well, one day Lady Harriet went into the tower so she would be able to watch all the horses as they ran by, but alas Lady Harriet fell from the tower and was trampled by all the horses and the ghost of Lady Harriet has haunted the tower and Wynnstay Park ever since."

". . . one of my mates went down to the column in the Wynnstay Park.

He heard that if you were to walk around the column three times then stop and listen you would hear a woman cry. People say that long ago a couple used to live there and one night the husband killed his wife by strangling her and the husband left and was never seen again."

". . . on a certain day (the 13th July or something like that) at 12 o'clock midnight with full moon, weird things happen. Some people say if you go round it ten times and knock on the door a woman with an axe is supposed to chase you into the woods."

I wonder if anyone's tried it!

Ruthin

Behind the 19th century Ruthin Castle, now a luxury hotel, famous for its medieval banquets, are the evocative ruins of the original castle, another of Edward I's Welsh chain of fortresses (see Rhuddlan). Its red sandstone walls reflect a bloody past. The castle was under the command of Reginald de Grey, whose arrogance towards the Welsh was largely responsible for the Glyndŵr uprising. A hint of de Grey's cruelty can be taken from the Drowning Pit, a small dungeon which would become flooded by the moat when a gate was raised. Here prisoners were put for de Grey's entertainment. The captive suffered an agonising death, struggling to keep his head above water until he was eventually drowned. The Whipping Pit, at the base of one of the towers, needs no elucidation.

In the light of such remnants of medieval horror, it seems surprising that the castle is today haunted by none but the peaceful presence of the Grey Lady, whose alleged grave can be found in a secluded corner of the battlements. She is believed to have been the wife of de Grey's second in command. She discovered her husband was having an affair with another woman — so promptly despatched her rival with an axe. When the dreadful deed was discovered, she was sentenced to death. Because she was a murderess, her body was buried in the battlements, rather than in consecrated ground, causing her restless spirit to wander for eternity. Dressed in a long grey gown, she is often encountered on the ramparts or most commonly in the medieval chapel, now the banqueting hall. Guests at the hotel can relax safe in the knowledge that her presence is an unthreatening one, and that she has never been seen with her axe — well, not yet!

An eerie and enigmatic apparition was seen by student Amanda Cooper in the summer of 1990 from a flat overlooking Well Street in the centre of Ruthin. She had been having a coffee with a friend late one night, when she chanced to look out of the window, and at once noticed "a strange figure, limping very badly, dragging its right leg, walking up Well Street towards the square."

Amanda continued: "It slowly made its way up the narrow pavement and came to the gap in the wall where the entrance to the Manor House is. It stopped here, turned and faced upwards, looking up towards the flat window. It was small, maybe five foot, and was wearing a light grey, drab cloak down to the ground and had a big, baggy hood covering its head. Where its face should have been was black. It carried on staring up for about thirty seconds."

Amanda had recognised there was something unearthly about the figure at once, and to her friend, whom she had quickly called over, she said, only half in jest: "I hope we're not seeing the Grim Reaper, because we're both for it if so!"

However, any fears of this sort were proved unfounded, as the apparition slowly turned away and walked down the path to the Manor House's main entrance, where it vanished. The girls were greatly frightened, and they can both recall the sighting vividly. However, to my knowledge this is an isolated incident, and the mysterious figure has certainly never been seen by either of the two girls again.

Hidden away in a little alcove in Ruthin Castle's ramparts is the Grey Lady's grave

Does the ghost of the murderous Grey Lady still use this old doorway on her nocturnal rambles round the ruins of Ruthin castle?

St Asaph

Christmas 1812 was not a peaceful one for the Roberts family of Bodeugan Farm, St Asaph. They were plagued by a poltergeist, which terrorised the household, making particular targets of the servant girls. A letter from farmer Robert Roberts to his lessor, Dr Currie of Chester, describing the spook's activities, is on file in the Clwyd Record Office at Hawarden, and makes fascinating reading. Beginning by apologising for his delay in sending geese for Dr Currie's Christmas table, Roberts explains the cause:

"We were troubled in the House that we could not attend to things as usual on the 1st Day of December at night Something began to break the windows by throwing stones and coals and other materials and did so the night following, we watch the two nights thinking it to be malicious persons but we found nothing the day after it began in the day time especially in the dairy to throw down the pots containing churning milk and breaking them to pieces and great many other earthenware and throwing cans and other things at us, but that night it was so terrible that the women left the house and went to a neighbour's house it threw stones bricks and the like that they had no quiet to milk by throwing dung upon them from noon a Thursday till Monday nothing was felt and it began on Monday the second time threw water and glasses at us that we were so wet as we had been in a river, and shifting many other things . . .

"It has ceased for 10 days after and began again on Saturday 24th Dec and it was more dangerous this time than before we went to bed about 10 o'clock Saturday night and began to kick and pincing the servants and pulling the bed clothes to the floor, and the two women along with them, and has done great deal of damage, and if it will continue we must leave the House my wife has frightened very much and she has been very ill but she is better at present but we cannot think now of other but that some malicious person or persons has been with some of the conjurers."

In response, Dr Currie sent Mr John Lloyd, curate of Llandrillo, and a colleague, Mr Hughes, to Bodeugan to investigate. They experienced nothing in the house, but as they were leaving, a farm worker called them back, saying something was happening in the dairy. There they found a servant girl washing some pots, which she said had just been "thrown down by some invisible power." A stick flew over Lloyd's head and struck Hughes. It had come from the direction of the girl and Hughes accused her of throwing it. She denied this, but Lloyd also thought he saw a potato coming from her hand, and then distinctly saw her throw a pepperpot to the floor. He accused her again: "but she told me 'she knew nothing of the potato or the pepperpot; but the Ghost might have made use of her hands to throw things'."

It is not unusual in poltergeist cases for people to unconsciously contribute to its destructive activities, so the girl may have been speaking the truth. Lloyd and Hughes went away convinced of her guilt, but Robert Roberts' father-in-law wrote to Dr Currie to assure him that this could not have been the case because when the poltergeist made a return in January, things occurred when the maids were full in view, and they were often the victims of attack. If a real poltergeist was behind the disturbances, one of the maids was likely to have been a focus, since an adolescent girl is commonly the centre of attention in modern cases. Here, sadly, the records end, but it can be assumed that the poltergeist continued harrassing the occupants of Bodeugan for a little while longer, and then, as these enigmatic entities tend to do, simply drifted away of its own accord and left them in peace.

Bodeugan Farm, St Asaph, plagued by a poltergeist in 1812

Shotton

Shotton on Deeside, like Brymbo, was once famous for its steelworks, and the little town grew up around them. The foundry was closed, but some production still continues, and I have heard that in recent years a most incongruous apparition was seen there — a little Victorian lady quietly going about her ironing in one of the old sheds!

Better authenticated is the lady who haunts an old schoolhouse in the town. The *Alyn and Deeside Observer* ran a story in 1977 about the ghost, which is apparently of a former occupant. Cynthia and Rob Furnivall, who lived in the house, described her as "a tall, well-made, middle-aged woman wearing a long, black 'Welsh lady' type of dress, with a small hat on the back of her dark, curly hair and a ribbon with a cameo round her neck." Their next door neighbour, who had lived there for 43 years, said this description fitted exactly that of a Mrs Henning, who had lived at the house during and after its time as a school. She is rarely seen but the Furnivalls would often feel her friendly presence about the place, most commonly in one of the bedrooms.

Trefnant

The shade of a road accident victim still hovers around the scene of his death on the outskirts of Trefnant, near Denbigh. He was encountered by Mr and Mrs Jones of Abergele, who told of their experience in a letter to my *History and Mystery* column in the *Denbighshire Free Press* newspaper. Explained the witnesses:

"It was a dusky evening and my husband and I were driving through Trefnant, when we saw the figure of a man wearing jacket and trousers walking along the other side by a very high hedge. As a big car was driving towards us, my husband steered into the hedge on our side to give it more room. The other driver swerved slightly round the figure, which suddenly vanished into the hedge. The other driver looked at us in disbelief and we shrugged our shoulders in amazement, showing that we too had seen it. The following day friends told us that a man had been killed there a few years before.

Unfortunately, Mr and Mrs Jones never discovered the identity of the other driver; it would have been interesting to have had a separate account of the incident from another witness.

Trelawnyd

The mysterious Gop Cairn, which looms above the village of Trelawnyd, near the coast, has been a puzzle to archaeologists for centuries. The second largest prehistoric man-made mound in Europe (the first being Silbury Hill in Wiltshire), the Cairn's purpose remains a mystery. Numerous excavations have shown that, despite its name, it is not a burial mound, and it is of insufficient size to have supported any kind of habitation. One suggestion is that it may once have served as the base for a beacon, but this is unlikely to have been its original function.

Whatever archaeology says, however, tradition maintains that the mound housed the burial of none other than the fierce warrior queen, Boudicca, herself. And this legend was given fresh colour in 1938, when a man walking from Diserth to Trelogan one night saw the field below Gop Cairn full of Roman soldiers! On Gop Hill a Roman general sat astride a white horse, brandishing a sword. The remarkable scene lasted only a few seconds. A cloud passed over the moon, all went dark, and the vision vanished.

Treuddyn

Ghost layer extraordinaire, the Rev. Griffiths, met with the most challenging exorcism of his career at Treuddyn, according to Jane Pugh in her *Welsh Ghostly Encounters*. An evil spirit had taken possession of the dairy at Ffrith Farm, throwing filth into the butter churns, hurling crockery around and attacking the terrified dairymaids with unseen hands. The farmer called in a priest to perform an exorcism, but the spirit showed its contempt for his efforts by waving a woman's bonnet in his face! Eventually, the Rev. Griffiths came to the rescue.

He went into the dairy and, as was his custom, drew two circles on the floor. He then charged the spirit to appear. It did so — in the form of lion! The beast roared at Griffiths and made to pounce upon him, but he knew that it could not leave its circle nor enter his. He told the entity that he would have nothing to do with it unless it appeared in a less alarming form. The spirit, which was apparently something of a show-off and enjoying the attention, then appeared as a huge black mastiff, saliva drooling from its jaws. But this, too, was unacceptable to Griffiths, and so a long battle of wits ensued. Outside in the churchyard, the farmer and his servants listened with awe as the dairy resounded to loud crashes and bloodcurdling screams. They were convinced Griffiths was being devoured by the demon!

However, despite their fears, the exorcist was at last successful. He convinced the spirit to make itself smaller and smaller, until it took on the harmless shape of a fly — at which point he scooped it up in one of his trusty tobacco tins and imprisoned it. He emerged from the dairy exhausted but triumphant. He said that the spirit was the most powerful he had ever faced. Having secured it, he then buried it, buzzing furiously in its tin prison, in a secret location, so that it would never trouble the mortal world again.

When Joe Kelly and Jane Walsh bought a little, wood-framed cottage in Treuddyn they found an unexpected free extra included in the deal — a large, Victorian Bible.

"Whatever you do, don't get rid of that Bible, it must stay in the house," the previous occupant warned them. Joe and Jane soon discovered that their new home, 'Stanscote,' had an unusual history. It was built at the end of the Great War by the parents of a young soldier, Stan, who was fighting in the trenches. Sadly, he did not live to take possession. Whether he died during the war, or shortly after, is uncertain, but his body is believed to be buried in the nearby churchyard. The Bible was placed in the cottage as soon as it was built, to welcome the returning hero, but was never removed. And it has remained there ever since, each successive occupant feeling it would be unlucky to sell it — particularly since Stan himself seems to be keeping an eye on it!

On occasions Stan's spirit seems to return to his intended home, to check that all is in order. A figure in an old-fashioned infantryman's uniform has several times been seen standing in the field at the bottom of the garden. He does not move, but simply stands and stares, and then vanishes. Joe and Jane have yet to encounter Stan's spirit, but they have experienced some eerie activity in the house: inexplicable noises and objects moving about and a bedroom door slamming open in the middle of the night with such force that it damaged the hinges. However, none of this perturbs the couple; on the contrary, Jane is delighted. She is a member of the Society for Psychical Research, and can't believe her luck that her new home is a haunted house!

Wrexham

Wrexham has the densest population in Clwyd, and therefore more likelihood of ghost sightings. The main town sprawls out and connects up with many satellite villages, most of which grew up with the mines exploiting the North East Wales Coalfield. Wrexham can boast perhaps more ghost stories than any other town its size anywhere in the country, rivalling even famed "ghost towns" like York, where hauntings have become one of the staples of its tourist industry. Sceptics might argue that this has something to do with the town's successful brewing industry — putting more than a few spooks down to the effects of Wrexham Lager! — but be that as it may, there are some fascinating stories and accounts to make even the hardened cynic shiver.

A premises in the High Street has long had a reputation for hauntings. The building was taken over by insurance brokers Barry Williams Associates in 1986, and after some refurbishment very strange things indeed started happening. Computer discs locked in a ground floor office at night were found in the morning scattered all over a room on the top floor. Unexpected chills and sudden periods of muggy warmth were experienced, while the thermometer registered a constant temperature. Filing cabinets jammed or opened as the mood took them, and then, a few days later, the most inexplicable phenomenon of all occurred — the word processor and photocopier started to leak water!

Every morning water would be found dripping from the machines or sometimes from the sockets they were plugged into. Electrical engineers were baffled — they could find no trace of water behind the sockets or in the plugs, and there was no indication of how it could find its way into the machines. There were no pipes nearby. One engineer simply wrote on his report card: "Weird!" Initially occurring at night, the leakages later began to take place in the early afternoon, thus doing away with the theory that they were down to some hoaxer — the machine stood in full view of everyone in the busy office.

The liquid would leave behind a milky residue, which was never identified, although it was taken away for analysis. Staff waited anxiously to see if some message would manifest on the word processor, but as is typical of so much inexplicable phenomena, it ended of its own accord, the mystery unsolved.

Mr Howard Fey, who had an office in the building — which was once a coach house — years before Barry Williams Associates, told *Evening Leader* reporter Tony Challis that he was not surprised by the phenomena: "A few times there I felt it cold, almost freezing, at the end of the building near the old stables. Several times I felt as if someone unseen was standing behind me. It was a quite extraordinary feeling. Stock-taking at night was always difficult on the High Street site. None of the staff would stay late."

Whilst reporting on the haunted word processor story, Mr Challis was informed of several other hauntings in nearby streets. Café owner Mr Herbert Marubbi, of Bank Street, told him: "We've got our own benign ghost. My kids have been brought up with him. His name is Billy Lloyd. He was a sadler in Charles Street. My mother used to cook his Sunday dinner and as a child I would take it to him and get a sixpence. He died on our premises. I took his dinner up one day and found him dead with his eyes open, which makes me think he wanted to come back."

And Mr Fred Gibson told of some frightening experiences at a three-storey house in Yorke Street in 1923, when he was a boy. The house was haunted by the ghost of an old man who had tripped and fallen down the stairs, smashing his oil lamp against the wall. The flaming oil burned the unfortunate man to death. The family would regularly be startled awake in the middle of the night by a loud crash and the sound of tinkling glass — with no apparent cause. One night Mr Gibson and his brother saw a candle hovering down the corridor with no visible means of support, and on another occasion Mr Gibson's uncle Alf, brother to their widowed mother, saw a man in a gown and mortar board come striding out of a wall, past the end of his bed and then through the opposite wall. The family left shortly afterwards. Enough, they decided, was enough!

Fire seems to have been the cause of another Wrexham haunting, in a shop in Charles Street. Parts of the building date back to 1627. It was once a pub, called the Green Man (a Pagan symbol) and later the Hat. The Hat was largely destroyed by fire at the turn of the century. Mr Sid Jones and his wife Dorothy, who used to live in a flat above the shop, believed that someone was killed in the blaze, and it was he who haunted the building.

During the night Mr and Mrs Jones would wake up at exactly the same time and see the room as if it were full of smoke. Through the haze the shadowy figure of a man could be seen. Their little boy once saw a strange man leaning over his bed. The phantom also manifested itself by producing strange noises in upstairs rooms, opening locked doors and causing the typical falls in temperature.

"We never believed the ghost would do us any harm," Mrs Jones told the *Evening Leader*. But there were times when it made them feel most unwelcome: "You could feel the apprehension growing — your spine would tingle," Mrs Jones explained. This usually occurred in the early evening, so, taking the hint, they would send their employees home early and lock up the shop, leaving the ghost to its privacy.

An ex-leather mill in Charles Street became the centre for poltergeist activity after a servant was walled up alive by his cruel master, according to Jane Pugh in her *Welsh Ghostly Encounters*. When the building later became used as a bakery, ovens would light up by themselves, loaves would burn and yeast and fresh bread would be spoilt. The activities quietened down, but a year or two ago, after some renovations, the entity made itself known again, scaring the residents of the two flats recently incorporated into the building. A heavy tread regularly paces the corridors, loud thuds echo from unknown corners of the building and knockings on doors are made by invisible hands.

While some interior decor was being carried out, an area of wall which had been blocked off was found. One of the residents took some measurements and worked out that a small area behind the wall and over the staircase did not correspond with the interior dimensions of the rooms — in short, a portion was left over. Is this the compartment in which an unfortunate man was walled in — the origin of the hauntings?

In her book, Jane Pugh also mentions a spirit being seen at midnight which holds out its arms in a gesture of blessing, a benign expression on its face. It appears near one of the main roundabouts in the town, built on the site of the martyrdom of Saint Richard Gwyn, who was hung, drawn and quartered in 1584 for his conversion to the Catholic faith. There are some who believe that this is an apparition of the saint himself. Sightings seem to have occurred only in recent years, so perhaps more developments are yet to come . . .

A trendy phantom monk recently took to haunting the Ferryman Nightclub in Abbot Street. Perhaps, after a lifetime of strict monastic denial, he was after a bit of fun — and where better than a disco? He did get a bit rowdy, however. Stools and glasses were moved about and once the barmaid felt her bottom pinched by an invisible hand. The ghost also enjoyed turning over the pages of a calendar when there was no-one about, just to cause confusion. Manager Mr Tony Green told the Press that staff blamed the strange activities on a ghostly monk who was said to have once haunted tunnels running under the club. Some became so frightened that they handed in their notices. Mr Green saw the apparition himself, entering one of the toilets at 3 a.m. Assuming at first that it was a customer, he followed, but inside found no-one there.

"I think we'll have to get the ghostbusters in to exorcise the place," he said.

An area of town with a history of ghostly goings on is Acton Park. Acton Hall, now demolished, was birthplace of the notorious "Hanging" Judge Jeffreys, and some believe that it is his misty form which has sometimes been seen patrolling the park. However, since the Judge lived for only a few years at the hall, and was mainly a visitor, this seems unlikely. Wrexham town guide Mrs Beryl Jones makes the more sensible suggestion that it is the shade of Sir Watkin Williams Wynn, who was killed in a riding accident in the park in 1749.

In 1982, one late Sunday night, 20-year-old Tim Davies was making his way through the park when he saw two white-robed figures enter the (modern) "Druid's Circle" from opposite ends. They met in the centre, clasped hands and danced within the circle — then vanished!

"I was so terrified I was rooted to the spot in fear for five minutes," he told the *Wrexham Leader*. "Then I ran home as fast as I could!"

The elegant National Trust-owned Erddig Hall, family home of the Yorke family, also has a reputation for being haunted, but reports are very vague. However, an account of a horrible vision — a spectre of a living person seen at the moment of death — is recorded in Albina Lucy Cust's *Chronicles of Erthig on the Dyke*, published in 1914. A Miss Massingham, aunt of Sir Joseph Yorke, was attending a musical recital in London on April 5, 1831, when she suddenly gave a terrible cry, startling the audience, and fainted dead away. She was carried out and revived. When she had recovered herself she told her companions that she had seen before her "the dripping form of a man, whose body was covered with a naval cloak." Although she could not see the face she was convinced it was the body of her nephew.

When she returned to Erddig she received the awful news that Joseph Yorke had been drowned in Southampton Water, along with two naval captains and a boatman, after their boat was overturned in a sudden squall of wind. The accident had occurred at about the time of Miss Massingham's vision . . .

Equally ghastly, but unidentified, apparitions were witnessed by two girls many years ago at the Cambrian Goodsyard, beside the old Cambrian Railway, at Caia Road. One of the girls, now Mrs E. M. Crowe, of Chester, told her story to the *Wrexham Leader*:

"One evening, whilst in our early teens, a cousin and myself went out delivering some butchers' aprons which an aunt had made for the town's tradesmen. It was quite late when we were returning home and at a spot between the railway and a corn merchant's warehouse, a strange object, legless, armless and faceless, came towards us; another, smaller, object appeared behind the first one. As we stared, rooted to the spot, they drifted past and suddenly disappeared into the wall of the railway bridge. We then realised that we had seen two ghosts."

Mrs Crowe believed these lumpy spectres were premonitions of the deaths, which took place shortly afterwards, of their next door neighbour, a tall man, and their grandfather, a short man. A fatal accident had taken place years previously at the goodsyard when a train, rounding the corner, shed its load of heavy flour bags onto the platform, crushing many people. Were the strange shapes floating flour bags?

Borras Hall is the setting for our last ghost story, and a real Gothic horror it is, too. I am indebted to Mrs Helen Bendon for pointing me in the direction of the tale, and to Mr John Parry, of Borras Hall, for the details. Mr Parry is sure the tale has no basis in fact, but my motto is never to let the facts get in the way of a good ghost story! The ghost of Borras Hall is said to be that of a past squire who suffered a most horrible and ignominious death centuries ago. The squire was a cruel man, very fond of hunting, who enjoyed beating his servants and was not averse to taking advantage of his defenceless maids. One afternoon, fate decided to take revenge on the squire's wickedness . . .

The squire was enjoying his favourite sport, foxhunting, and was

Borras Hall

looking forward to the kill. Mounted on his best charger, he surveyed the country from a high slope near the hall as below him his hounds sniffed and bayed around a spinney in which the fox was holed up. Suddenly, for some unknown reason, his horse reared, and the squire was thrown. He fell a very many feet through the air, crashing into a tree which grew at the foot of the slope. He plunged downwards through the branches, until his head caught in the fork of a bough. Such was his momentum, the squire's head was ripped from his shoulders. His decapitated body fell at the foot of the tree, but his head bounced several times on the grass — and then rolled straight into the pack of hounds! The bloodlust upon them, the pack were delighted with this unexpected morsel and, their attention drawn momentarily from their quarry, they tucked in for a feast.

The master of the hounds tried to pull the dogs back, but he was too late. By the time he had forced his way amongst them, there was scarcely a scrap left. The hounds had eaten their master's head right down to the last mouthful!

Bibliography

Barber, Chris, *Ghosts of Wales, Mysterious Wales*
Baring-Gould, S., *A Book of North Wales*
Bartlett, Michael, *Britain's Most Haunted Places*
Black, I. D., *The Story of Mancot*
Bord, Janet and Colin, *Modern Mysteries of the World*
Bradley, A. G., *Highways and Byways in North Wales, The Romance of Wales*
Clough, M. B., *Scenes and Stories Little Known*
Coleman, S. J., *Legendary Lore of Denbighshire*
Coulter, Stan, *The Rhewl*
Cust, Albina Lucy, *Chronicles of Erthig on the Dyke*
Davies, Ellis, *Prehistoric and Roman Remains of Flintshire*
Fraser, Maxwell, *Wales Vol 2*
Jarman, Sydney G., *Rossett and Marford*
Jones, Brian and Rawcliffe, Margaret, *Llanddulas*
Leslie, Charles Henry, *Rambles Round Mold*
Longrigg, G. H., *Legends of the Dee*
Morgan, Rev. J. J., *A welais ac a Glywais*
Owen, Rev. Elias, *Welsh Folklore, Old Stone Crosses of the Vale of Clwyd*
"Penman", *'Mold Gleanings'* (from *Chester Chronicle*)
Pennant, Thomas, *A Tour Through Wales*
Playfair, Guy Lion, *The Haunted Pub Guide*
Pugh, Jane, *Welsh Ghosts, Poltergeists and Demons, Welsh Ghostly Encounters*
Radford, Ken, *Tales of North Wales*
Sikes, Wirt, *British Goblins*
Trevelyan, Marie, *Folklore and Folk Stories of Wales*
Underwood, Peter, *Ghosts of Wales*
Williams, J. Gwynn, *Witchcraft in 17th Century Flintshire* (Flintshire Historical Society Transactions)
Welsh Legends
Llangynhafal, a Parish and its Past
Evening Leader

Flintshire Leader
Wrexham Leader
Denbighshire Free Press
North Wales Pioneer
North Wales Newsline
Bye-gones (from Oswestry and Border Counties Advertizer)
The Chronicle
Alyn and Deeside Observer
Country Quest